THE KENTUCKY-VIRGINIA RESOLUTIONS

AND

MR. MADISON'S REPORT OF 1799

THE
KENTUCKY-VIRGINIA
RESOLUTIONS

AND
MR. MADISON'S REPORT
OF 1799

Reprinted and distributed as a public service by THE VIRGINIA COMMISSION ON CONSTITUTIONAL GOVERNMENT, as the third in a series of vital statements on State and Federal relations.

IN the summer of 1798, a Federalist-dominated Congress of the United States passed three laws relating to aliens. These were harsh and tyrannical laws, politically motivated by a desire to control the flow of European immigrants who might be attracted to Jeffersonian standards. One of the statutes permitted the President, on his unchecked whim, to deport any alien he alone judged "dangerous to the peace or safety of the United States."

These were accompanied by an act still more oppressive, the Sedition Act of July 14, 1798. In the very teeth of the First Amendment's command that Congress pass no law abridging the freedom of the press, the Congress passed a law making it a criminal offense for any person to print "any false, scandalous and malicious writings against the government of the United States." The law prohibited any publication that might "excite the hatred of the good people of the United States" against Congress or the President. It was made unlawful for anyone even to urge opposition to any act of the President, or to urge the defeat of an act of Congress.

By contemporary standards, the Sedition Act especially must be viewed as an incredible offense against the Constitution. Yet Supreme Court justices of that day—Paterson, Chase and Bushrod Washington—repeatedly upheld the law, and saw that men were sentenced to prison for its violation. The light of individual freedom, raised at such sacrifice only a few years before, burned terribly dim. Neither the President, nor the Congress, nor the Supreme Court comprehended the evil here afoot.

In this crisis of constitutional government, Jefferson and Madison arranged for adoption of the famed Kentucky and Virginia Resolutions. Here, the General Assemblies of the two States enunciated in clear and vigorous language the right and duty of the States to intercede against a palpable and dangerous violation of the Constitution in order "to arrest the progress of the evil." The two resolutions were followed by Mr. Madison's Report of 1799, amplifying the position taken in Virginia a year earlier, and by a second resolution in Kentucky.

The student of constitutional government can find few starting points better suited for his inquiries than these profound statements on the meaning and structure of constitutional union.

The Virginia Commission on Constitutional
Government, Richmond, Virginia

March, 1960.

JK
176
1960

THE KENTUCKY-VIRGINIA RESOLUTIONS

AND

MR. MADISON'S REPORT OF 1799

☆ ☆ ☆ ☆ ☆ ☆ ☆ ☆ ☆ ☆ ☆ ☆ ☆

THE
KENTUCKY-VIRGINIA
RESOLUTIONS AND
MR. MADISON'S REPORT OF 1799

KENTUCKY LEGISLATURE

in the House of Representatives

November 10th, 1798.

RESOLVED, that the several States composing the United States of America, are not united on the principles of unlimited submission to their General Government; but that by compact under the style and title of a Constitution for the United States and of amendments thereto, they constituted a General Government for special purposes, delegated to that Government certain definite powers, reserving each State to itself, the residuary mass of right to their own self Government; and that whensoever the General Government assumes undelegated powers, its acts are unauthoritative, void, and of no force: That to this compact each State acceded as a State, and is an integral party, its co-States forming as to itself, the other party: That the Government created by this compact was not made the exclusive or final *judge* of the extent of the powers delegated to itself; since that would have made its discretion, and not the Constitution, the measure of its powers; but that as in all other cases of compact among parties having no common Judge, each party has an equal right to judge for itself, as well of infractions as of the mode and measure of redress.

II. Resolved, that the Constitution of the United States having delegated to Congress a power to punish treason, counterfeiting the securities and current coin of the United States, piracies and felonies committed on the High Seas, and offenses against the laws of nations, and no other crimes whatever, and it being true as a general principle, and one of the amendments to the Constitution having also declared, "that the powers not delegated to the United States by the Constitution, nor prohibited by it to the States, are reserved to the States respectively, or to the people," therefore also the same act of Congress passed on the 14th day of July, 1798, and entitled "An act in addition to the act entitled an act for the punishment of certain crimes against the United States," as also the act passed by them on the 27th day of June, 1798, entitled "An act to punish frauds committed on the Bank of the United States" (and all other their acts which assume to create, define, or punish crimes other than those enumerated in the Constitution) are altogether void and of no force, and that the power to create, define, and punish such other crimes is reserved, and of right appertains solely and exclusively to the respective States, each within its own Territory.

III. Resolved, that it is true as a general principle, and is also expressly declared by one of the amendments to the Constitution that "the powers not delegated to the United States by the Constitution, nor prohibited by it to the States, are reserved to the States respectively or to the people;" and that no power over the freedom of religion, freedom of speech, or freedom of the press being delegated to the United States by the Constitution, nor prohibited by it to the States, all lawful powers respecting the same did of right remain, and were reserved to the States, or to the people: That thus was manifested their determination to retain to themselves the right of judging how far the licentiousness of speech and of the press may be abridged without lessening their useful freedom, and how far those abuses which cannot be separated from their use, should be tolerated rather than the use be destroyed; and thus also they guarded against all abridgement by the United States of the freedom of religious opinions and exercises, and retained to themselves the right of protecting the same, as this state by a Law passed on the general demand of its Citizens, had already protected them from all human restraint or inteference: And that in addition to this general principle and express declaration, another and more special provision has been made by one of the amendments to the Constitution which expressly declares, that "Congress shall make no law respecting an Establishment of religion, or prohibiting the free exercise thereof, or abridging the freedom of speech, or the press," thereby guarding in the same sentence, and under the same words, the freedom of religion, of speech, and of the press, insomuch, that whatever violates either, throws down the sanctuary which covers the others, and that libels, falsehoods, and defamation, equally with heresy and false religion, are withheld from the cognizance of federal tribunals. That therefore the act of the Congress of the United States passed on the 14th day of July 1798, entitled "An act in addition to the act for the punishment of certain crimes against the United States," which does abridge the freedom of the press, is not law, but is altogether void and of no effect.

IV. Resolved, that alien friends are under the jurisdiction

and protection of the laws of the State wherein they are; that no power over them has been delegated to the United States, nor prohibited to the individual States distinct from their power over citizens; and it being true as a general principle, and one of the amendments to the Constitution having also declared, that "the powers not delegated to the United States by the Constitution nor prohibited by it to the States are reserved to the States respectively or to the people," the act of the Congress of the United States passed on the 22d day of June, 1798, entitled "An act concerning aliens," which assumes power over alien friends not delegated by the Constitution, is not law, but is altogether void and of no force.

V. Resolved, that in addition to the general principle as well as the express declaration, that powers not delegated are reserved, another and more special provision inserted in the Constitution from abundant caution has declared, "that the *migration* or importation of such persons as any of the States now existing shall think proper to admit, shall not be prohibited by the Congress prior to the year 1808." That this Commonwealth does admit the migration of alien friends described as the subject of the said act concerning aliens; that a provision against prohibiting their migration, is a provision against all acts equivalent thereto, or it would be nugatory; that to remove them when migrated is equivalent to a prohibition of their migration, and is therefore contrary to the said provision of the Constitution and void.

VI. Resolved, that the imprisonment of a person under the protection of the Laws of this Commonwealth on his failure to obey the simple *order* of the President to depart out of the United States, as is undertaken by the said act entitled "An act concerning Aliens," is contrary to the Constitution, one amendment to which has provided, that "no person shall be deprived of liberty without due process of law," and that

4

another having provided "that in all criminal prosecutions, the accused shall enjoy the right to a public trial by an impartial jury, to be informed of the nature and cause of the accusation, to be confronted with the witnesses against him, to have compulsory process for obtaining witnesses in his favour, and to have the assistance of counsel for his defence," the same act undertaking to authorize the President to remove a person out of the United States who is under the protection of the Law, on his own suspicion, without accusation, without jury, without public trial, without confrontation of the witnesses against him, without having witnesses in his favour, without defence, without counsel, is contrary to these provisions also of the Constitution, is therefore not law but utterly void and of no force.

That transferring the power of judging any person who is under the protection of the laws, from the Courts to the President of the United States, as is undertaken by the same act concerning Aliens, is against the article of the Constitution which provides, that "the judicial power of the United States shall be vested in Courts, the Judges of which shall hold their offices during good behaviour," and that the said act is void for that reason also; and it is further to be noted, that this transfer of Judiciary power is to that magistrate of the General Government who already possesses all the Executive, and a qualified negative in all the Legislative powers.

VII. Resolved, that the construction applied by the General Government (as is evinced by sundry of their proceedings) to those parts of the Constitution of the United States which delegate to Congress a power to lay and collect taxes, duties, imposts, and excises; to pay the debts, and provide for the common defence, and general welfare of the United States, and to make all laws which shall be necessary and proper for carrying into execution the powers vested by the Constitution in the Government of the United States, or any department thereof, goes to the destruction of all the limits prescribed to their power by the Constitution—That words meant by that instrument to be subsiduary only to the execution of the limited powers, ought not to be so construed as themselves to give unlimited powers, nor a part so to be taken, as to destroy the whole residue of the instrument: That the proceedings of the General Government under colour of these articles, will be a fit and necessary subject for revisal and correction at a time of greater tranquility, while those specified in the preceding resolutions call for immediate redress.

VIII. Resolved, that the preceeding Resolutions be transmitted to the Senators and Representatives in Congress from this Commonwealth, who are hereby enjoined to present the same to their respective Houses, and to use their best endeavours to procure at the next session of Congress, a repeal of the aforesaid unconstitutional and obnoxious acts.

IX. Resolved lastly, that the Governor of this Commonwealth be, and is hereby authorised and requested to communicate the preceding Resolutions to the Legislatures of the several States, to assure them that this Commonwealth considers Union for specified National purposes, and particularly for those specified in their late Federal Compact, to be friendly to the peace, happiness, and prosperity of all the States: that faithful to that compact, according to the plain intent and meaning in which it was understood and acceded to by the several parties, it is sincerely anxious for its preservation: that it does also believe, that to take from the States all the powers of self government, and transfer them to a general and consolidated Government, without regard to the special delegations and reservations solemnly agreed to in that compact, is not for the peace, happiness, or prosperity of these States: And that therefore, this Commonwealth is determined, as it doubts not its co-States are, tamely to submit to undelegated & consequently unlimited powers in no man or body of men on earth: that if the acts before specified should stand, these conclusions would flow from them; that the General Government may place any act they think proper on the list of crimes & punish it themselves, whether enumerated or not enumerated by the Constitution as cognizable by them: that they may transfer its cognizance to the President or any other person, who may himself be the accuser, counsel, judge, and jury, whose *suspicions* may be the evidence, his order the sentence, his officer the executioner, and his breast the sole record of the transaction: that a very numerous and valuable description of the inhabitants of these States, being by this precedent reduced as outlaws to the absolute dominion of one man and the barrier of the Constitution thus swept away from us all, no rampart now remains against the passions and the power of a majority of Congress, to protect from a like exportation or other more grievous punishment the minority of the same body, the Legislatures, Judges, Governors, & Counsellors of the States, nor their other peaceable inhabitants who may venture to reclaim the constitutional rights & liberties of the States & people, or who for other causes, good or bad, may be obnoxious to the views or marked by the suspicions of the President, or be thought dangerous to his or their elections or other interests public or personal: that the friendless alien has indeed been selected as the safest subject of a first experiment: but the citizen will soon follow, or rather has already followed; for, already has a Sedition Act marked him as its prey: that these and successive acts of the same character, unless arrested on the threshold, may tend to drive these States into revolution and blood, and will furnish new calumnies against Republican Governments, and new pretexts for those who wish it to be believed, that man cannot be governed but by a rod of iron: that it would be a dangerous delusion were a confidence in the men of our choice to silence our fears for the safety of our rights: that confidence is every where the parent of despotism: free government is founded in jealousy and not in confidence; it is jealousy and not confidence which prescribes limited Constitutions to bind down those whom we are obliged to trust with power: that our Constitution has accordingly fixed the limits to which and no further our confidence may go; and let the honest advocate of confidence read the Alien and Sedition Acts, and say if the Constitution has not been wise in fixing limits to the Government it created, and whether we should be wise in destroying those limits? Let him say what the Government is if it be not a tyranny, which the men of our choice have conferred on the President, and the President of our choice has assented to and accepted over the friendly strangers, to whom the mild spirit of our Country and its laws had pledged hospitality and protection: that the men of our choice have more respected the bare suspicions of the President than the solid rights of innocence, the claims of justification, the sacred force of truth, and the forms & substance of law and justice. In questions of power then let no more be heard of confidence in man, but bind him down from mischief by the chains of the Constitution. That this Commonwealth does therefore call on its co-States for an expression of their sentiments on the acts concerning Aliens, and for the punishment of certain crimes herein before specified, plainly declaring whether these acts are or are not authorized by the Federal Compact? And it doubts not that their sense will be so announced as to prove their attachment unaltered to limited Government, whether general or particular, and that the rights and liberties of their co-States will be exposed to no dangers by remaining embarked on a common bottom with their own: That they will

8

concur with this Commonwealth in considering the said acts as so palpably against the Constitution as to amount to an undisguised declaration, that the Compact is not meant to be the measure of the powers of the General Government, but that it will proceed in the exercise over these States of all powers whatsoever: That they will view this as seizing the rights of the States and consolidating them in the hands of the General Government with a power assumed to bind the States (not merely in cases made federal) but in all cases whatsoever, by laws made, not with their consent, but by others against their consent: That this would be to surrender the form of Government we have chosen, and to live under one deriving its powers from its own will, and not from our authority; and that the co-States recurring to their natural right in cases not made federal, will concur in declaring these acts void and of no force, and will each unite with this Commonwealth in requesting their repeal at the next session of Congress.

EDMUND BULLOCK, S. H. R.
JOHN CAMPBELL, S. S. P. T.

Passed the House of Representatives, Nov. 10th, 1798.
   Attest,

THOMAS TODD, C. H. R.

In SENATE, *November 13th, 1798, unanimously*
                    concurred in,
   Attest,   B. THRUSTON, *Clk. Sen.*

Approved November 16th, 1798.

JAMES GARRARD, G. K.

By THE GOVERNOR,

HARRY TOULMIN,
Secretary of State.

9

THE GENERAL ASSEMBLY OF VIRGINIA

in the House of Delegates

RESOLVED, That the General Assembly of Virginia, doth unequivocally express a firm resolution to maintain and defend the Constitution of the United States, and the Constitution of this State, against every aggression either foreign or domestic, and that they will support the government of the United States in all measures warranted by the former.

That this Assembly most solemnly declares a warm attachment to the Union of the States, to maintain which it pledges all its powers; and that for this end, it is their duty to watch over and oppose every infraction of those principles which constitute the only basis of that Union, because a faithful observance of them, can alone secure its existence and the public happiness.

That this Assembly doth explicitly and peremptorily declare, that it views the powers of the federal government, as resulting from the compact, to which the States are parties; as limited by the plain sense and intention of the instrument constituting that compact; as no further valid than they are authorized by the grants enumerated in that compact; and that in case of a deliberate, palpable, and dangerous exercise of other powers, not granted by the said compact, the States who are parties thereto, have the right, and are in duty bound, to interpose for arresting the progress of the evil, and for maintaining within their respective limits, the authorities, rights and liberties appertaining to them.

That the General Assembly doth also express its deep regret, that a spirit has in sundry instances, been manifested by the federal government, to enlarge its powers by forced constructions of the constitutional charter which defines them; and that indications have appeared of a design to expound certain general phrases (which having been copied from the very limited grant of powers in the former articles of confederation were the less liable to be misconstrued) so as to destroy the meaning and effect, of the particular enumeration which necessarily explains and limits the general phrases; and so as to consolidate the States by degrees, into one sovereignty, the obvious tendency and inevitable consequence of which would be, to transform the present republican system of the United States, into an absolute, or at best a mixed monarchy.

That the General Assembly doth particularly protest against the palpable and alarming infractions of the Constitution, in the two late cases of the "Alien and Sedition Acts" passed at the last session of Congress; the first of which exercises a power nowhere delegated to the federal government, and which by uniting legislative and judicial powers to those of executive, subverts the general principles of free government, as well as the particular organization, and positive provisions of the federal Constitution; and the other of which acts, exercises in like manner, a power not delegated by the Constitution, but on the contrary, expressly and positively forbidden by one of the amendments thereto;—a power, which more than any other, ought to produce universal alarm, because it is leveled against that right of freely examining public characters and measures, and of free communication among the people thereon, which has ever been justly deemed, the only effectual guardian of every other right.

11

That this State having by its Convention, which ratified the Federal Constitution, expressly declared, that among other essential rights, "the Liberty of Conscience and of the Press cannot be cancelled, abridged, restrained, or modified by any authority of the United States," and from its extreme anxiety to guard these rights from every possible attack of sophistry or ambition, having with other States, recommended an amendment for that purpose, which amendment was, in due time, annexed to the Constitution; it would mark a reproachful inconsistency, and criminal degeneracy, if an indifference were now shewn, to the most palpable violation of one of the Rights, thus declared and secured; and to the establishment of a precedent which may be fatal to the other.

That the good people of this Commonwealth, having ever felt, and continuing to feel, the most sincere affection for their brethren of the other States; the truest anxiety for establishing and perpetuating the union of all; and the most scrupulous fidelity to that Constitution, which is the pledge of mutual friendship, and the instrument of mutual happiness, the General Assembly doth solemnly appeal to the like dispositions of the other States, in confidence that they will concur with this Commonwealth in declaring, as it does hereby declare, that the acts aforesaid, are unconstitutional; and that the necessary and proper measures will be taken by each, for cooperating with this State, in maintaining the Authorities, Rights, and Liberties, reserved to the States respectively, or to the People.

That the Governor be desired, to transmit a copy of the foregoing Resolutions to the executive authority of each of the other States, with a request that the same may be communicated to the Legislature thereof; and that a copy be furnished to each of the Senators and Representatives representing this State in the Congress of the United States.

Agreed to by the Senate, December 24, 1798.

KENTUCKY LEGISLATURE

in the House of Representatives

November 14th, 1799.

RESOLVED, That this Commonwealth considers the federal Union, upon the terms and for the purposes specified in the late compact, conducive to the liberty and happiness of the several States: That it does now unequivocally declare its attachment to the Union, and to that compact, agreeably to its obvious and real intention, and will be among the last to seek its dissolution: That, if those who administer the General Government be permitted to transgress the limits fixed by that compact, by a total disregard to the special delegations of power therein contained, an annihilation of the State Governments, and the creation upon their ruins, of a General Consolidated Government, will be the inevitable consequence: That the principle and construction contended for by sundry of the State legislatures, that the General Government is the exclusive judge of the extent of the powers delegated to it, stop nothing short of *despotism*—since the discretion of those who administer the government, and not the *Constitution,* would be the measure of their powers: That the several States who formed that instrument being sovereign and independent, have the unquestionable right to judge of the infraction; and *That a Nullification by those sovereignties, of all unauthorized acts done under color of that instrument is the rightful remedy:* That this Commonwealth does, under the most deliberate reconsideration, declare, that the said Alien and Sedition Laws are, in their opinion, palpable violations of the said Constitution: and, however cheerfully it may be disposed to surrender its opinion to a majority of its sister States, in matters of ordinary or doubtful policy, yet, in momentous regulations like the present, which so vitally wound the best rights of the citizen, it would consider a silent acquiescence as highly criminal: That, although this Commonwealth, as a party to the federal compact, will bow to the laws of the Union, yet, it does, at the same time declare, that it will not now, or ever hereafter, cease to oppose in a constitutional manner, every attempt at what quarter soever offered, to violate that compact. And, finally, in order that no pretext or arguments may be drawn from a supposed acquiescence, on the part of this Commonwealth in the constitutionality of these laws, and be thereby used as precedents for similar future violations of the federal compact—this Commonwealth does now enter against them its solemn PROTEST.

Attest,

THOMAS TODD, C.H.R.

In SENATE, *Nov. 22, 1799.*
  Attest,

B. THRUSTON, C.S.

THE GENERAL ASSEMBLY OF VIRGINIA

in the House of Delegates

Tuesday, January 7, 1800.

THE House according to the order of the day, resolved itself into a committee of the whole House, on the report of the committee to whom was committed the proceedings of sundry of the other States in answer to the resolutions of the General Assembly of the 21st day of December, 1798, and after some time spent therein, Mr. Speaker resumed the chair, and Mr. Mercer reported, that the committee of the whole House had, according to order, had the said report under their consideration, and had made an amendment thereto, which he read in his place, and then delivered in at the clerk's table where the same was again twice read, and agreed to by the House.

The said report as amended, is as follows:

Whatever room might be found in the proceedings of some of the States, who have disapproved of the resolutions of the General Assembly of this Commonwealth, passed on the 21st day of December, 1798, for painful remarks on the spirit and manner of those proceedings, it appears to the committee, most consistent with the duty, as well as dignity of the General Assembly, to hasten an oblivion of every circumstance, which might be construed into a diminution of mutual respect, confidence and affection, among the members of the union.

The committee have deemed it a more useful task, to revise

15

with a critical eye, the resolutions which have met with this disapprobation; to examine fully the several objections and arguments which have appeared against them; and to enquire, whether there be any errors of fact, of principle, or of reasoning, which the candour of the General Assembly ought to acknowledge and correct.

The first of the resolutions is in the words following:

Resolved, that the General Assembly of Virginia, doth unequivocally express a firm resolution to maintain and defend the Constitution of the United States, and the Constitution of this State, against every aggression either foreign or domestic, and that they will support the government of the United States in all measures warranted by the former.

No unfavorable comment can have been made on the sentiments here expressed. To maintain and defend the Constitution of the United States, and of their own State, against every aggression both foreign and domestic, and to support the government of the United States in all measures warranted by their constitution, are duties, which the General Assembly ought always to feel, and to which on such an occasion, it was evidently proper to express their sincere and firm adherence.

In their next resolution—*The General Assembly most solemnly declares a warm attachment to the union of the States, to maintain which, it pledges all its powers; and that for this end, it is their duty to watch over and oppose every infraction of those principles, which constitute the only basis of that union, because a faithful observance of them, can alone secure its existence and the public happiness.*

The observation just made is equally applicable to this solemn declaration, of warm attachment to the union, and this solemn pledge to maintain it: nor can any question arise among enlightened friends of the union, as to the duty of watching over and opposing every infraction of those principles which constitute its basis, and a faithful observance of which, can alone secure its existence, and the public happiness thereon depending.

The third resolution is in the words following:

That this Assembly doth explicitly and peremptorily declare, that it views the powers of the Federal Government, as resulting from the compact, to which the States are parties, as limited by the plain sense and intention of the instrument constituting that compact; as no farther valid than they are authorized by the grants enumerated in that compact; and that in case of a deliberate, palpable *and* dangerous *exercise of other powers, not granted by the said compact, the states who are parties thereto, have the right, and are in duty bound, to interpose, for arresting the progress of the evil, and for maintaining within their respective limits, the authorities, rights and liberties appertaining to them.*

On this resolution, the committee have bestowed all the attention which its importance merits: They have scanned it not merely with a strict, but with a severe eye; and they feel confidence in pronouncing, that in its just and fair construction, it is unexceptionably true in its several positions, as well as constitutional and conclusive in its inferences.

The resolution declares, *first*, that "it views the powers of the Federal Government, as resulting from the compact to which the States are parties," in other words, that the federal powers are derived from the Constitution, and that the Constitution is a compact to which the states are parties.

Clear as the position must seem, that the federal powers are derived from the Constitution, and from that alone, the committee are not unapprized of a late doctrine which opens another source of federal powers, not less extensive and important, than it is new and unexpected. The examination of this doctrine will be most conveniently connected with a review of a succeeding resolution. The committee satisfy themselves here with briefly remarking, that in all the co-temporary discussions and comments, which the Constitution underwent, it was constantly justified and recommended on the ground, that the powers not given to the government, were withheld from it; and that if any doubt could have existed on this subject, under the original text of the Constitution, it is removed as far as words could remove it, by the [TENTH] Amendment, now a part of the Constitution, which expressly declares, "that the powers not delegated to the United States, "by the Constitution, nor prohibited by it to the States, are "reserved to the States respectively, or to the people."

The other position involved in this branch of the resolution, namely, "that the States are parties to the Constitution or compact," is in the judgment of the committee, equally free from objection. It is indeed true that the term "States," is sometimes used in a vague sense, and sometimes in different senses, according to the subject to which it is applied. Thus it sometimes means the separate sections of territory occupied by the political societies within each; sometimes the particular governments, established by those societies; sometimes those societies as organized into those particular governments; and lastly, it means the people composing those political societies, in their highest sovereign capacity. Although it might be wished that the perfection of language admitted less diversity in the signification of the same words, yet little inconveniency is produced by it, where the true sense can be collected with certainty from the different applications. In the present instance whatever different constructions of the term "States," in the resolution may have been entertained, all will at least concur in that last mentioned; because in that sense, the Con-

18

stitution was submitted to the "States:" In that sense the "States" ratified it; and in that sense of the term "States," they are consequently parties to the compact from which the powers of the Federal government result.

The next position is, that the General Assembly views the powers of the Federal government, "as limited by the plain sense and intention of the instrument constituting that compact," and "as no farther valid than they are authorized by the grants therein enumerated." It does not seem possible that any just objection can lie against either of these clauses. The first amounts merely to a declaration that the compact ought to have the interpretation, plainly intended by the parties to it; the other, to a declaration, that it ought to have the execution and effect intended by them. If the powers granted, be valid, it is solely because they are granted; and if the granted powers are valid, because granted, all other powers not granted, must not be valid.

The resolution having taken this view of the federal compact, proceeds to infer, "that in case of a deliberate, palpable, and dangerous exercise of other powers not granted by the said compact, the States who are parties thereto, have the right, and are in duty bound to interpose for arresting the progress of the evil, and for maintaining within their respective limits, the authorities, rights and liberties appertaining to them."

It appears to your committee to be a plain principle, founded in common sense, illustrated by common practice, and essential to the nature of compacts; that where resort can be had to no tribunal superior to the authority of the parties, the parties themselves must be the rightful judges in the last resort, whether the bargain made, has been pursued or violated. The Constitution of the United States was formed by the sanction of the States, given by each in its sovereign capacity. It adds

19

to the stability and dignity, as well as to the authority of the Constitution, that it rests on this legitimate and solid foundation. The States then being the parties to the constitutional compact, and in their sovereign capacity, it follows of necessity, that there can be no tribunal above their authority, to decide in the last resort, whether the compact made by them be violated; and consequently that as the parties to it, they must themselves decide in the last resort, such questions as may be of sufficient magnitude to require their interposition.

It does not follow, however, that because the States as sovereign parties to their constitutional compact, must ultimately decide whether it has been violated, that such a decision ought to be interposed either in a hasty manner, or on doubtful and inferior occasions. Even in the case of ordinary conventions between different nations, where, by the strict rule of interpretation, a breach of a part may be deemed a breach of the whole; every part being deemed a condition of every other part, and of the whole, it is always laid down that the breach must be both wilful and material to justify an application of the rule. But in the case of an intimate and constitutional union, like that of the United States, it is evident that the interposition of the parties, in their sovereign capacity, can be called for by occasions only, deeply and essentially affecting the vital principles of their political system.

The resolution has accordingly guarded against any misapprehension of its object, by expressly requiring for such an interposition "the case of a *deliberate, palpable* and *dangerous* breach of the Constitution, by the exercise of *powers not granted* by it. It must be a case, not of a light and transient nature, but of a nature *dangerous* to the great purposes for which the Constitution was established. It must be a case moreover not obscure or doubtful in its construction, but plain and *palpable*. Lastly, it must be a case not resulting from a partial

20

consideration, or hasty determination; but a case stampt with a final consideration and *deliberate* adherence. It is not necessary because the resolution does not require, that the question should be discussed, how far the exercise of any particular power, ungranted by the Constitution, would justify the interposition of the parties to it. As cases might easily be stated, which none would contend, ought to fall within that description: Cases, on the other hand, might, with equal ease, be stated, so flagrant and so fatal as to unite every opinion in placing them within the description.

But the resolution has done more than guard against misconstruction, by expressly referring to cases of a *deliberate, palpable* and *dangerous* nature. It specifies the object of the interposition which it contemplates, to be solely that of arresting the progress of the *evil* of usurpation, and of maintaining the authorities, rights and liberties appertaining to the States, as parties to the Constitution.

From this view of the resolution, it would seem inconceivable that it can incur any just disapprobation from those, who laying aside all momentary impressions, and recollecting the genuine source and object of the Federal Constitution, shall candidly and accurately interpret the meaning of the General Assembly. If the deliberate exercise, of dangerous powers, palpably withheld by the Constitution, could not justify the parties to it, in interposing even so far as to arrest the progress of the evil, and thereby to preserve the Constitution itself as well as to provide for the safety of the parties to it; there would be an end to all relief from usurped power, and a direct subversion of the rights specified or recognized under all the State constitutions, as well as a plain denial of the fundamental principle on which our independence itself was declared.

But it is objected that the judicial authority is to be regarded as the sole expositor of the Constitution, in the last resort; and it may be asked for what reason, the declaration by the General Assembly, supposing it to be theoretically true, could be required at the present day and in so solemn a manner.

On this objection it might be observed *first*, that there may be instances of usurped power, which the forms of the Constitution would never draw within the control of the Judicial Department: secondly, that if the decision of the judiciary be raised above the authority of the sovereign parties to the Constitution, the decisions of the other departments, not carried by the forms of the Constitution before the judiciary, must be equally authoritative and final with the decisions of that department. But the proper answer to the objection is, that the resolution of the General Assembly relates to those great and extraordinary cases, in which all the forms of the Constitution may prove ineffectual against infractions dangerous to the essential rights of the parties to it. The resolution supposes that dangerous powers not delegated, may not only be usurped and executed by the other departments, but that the Judicial Department also may exercise or sanction dangerous powers beyond the grant of the Constitution; and consequently that the ultimate right of the parties to the Constitution, to judge whether the compact has been dangerously violated, must extend to violations by one delegated authority, as well as by another; by the judiciary, as well as by the executive, or the legislature.

However true therefore it may be that the Judicial Department, is, in all questions submitted to it by the forms of the Constitution, to decide in the last resort, this resort must necessarily be deemed the last in relation to the authorities of the other departments of the government; not in relation to the rights of the parties to the constitutional compact, from which the judicial as well as the other departments hold their delegated trusts. On any other hypothesis, the delegation of judicial power, would annul the authority delegating it; and the concurrence of this department with the others in usurped powers, might subvert forever, and beyond the possible reach of any rightful remedy, the very Constitution, which all were instituted to preserve.

The truth declared in the resolution being established, the expediency of making the declaration at the present day, may safely be left to the temperate consideration and candid judgment of the American public. It will be remembered that a frequent recurrence to fundamental principles is solemnly enjoined by most of the State constitutions, and particularly by our own, as a necessary safeguard against the danger of degeneracy to which republics are liable, as well as other governments, though in a less degree than others. And a fair comparison of the political doctrines not unfrequent at the present day, with those which characterized the epoch of our revolution, and which form the basis of our republican constitutions, will best determine whether the declaratory recurrence here made to those principles ought to be viewed as unseasonable and improper, or as a vigilant discharge of an important duty. The authority of constitutions over governments, and of the sovereignty of the people over constitutions, are truths which are at all times necessary to be kept in mind; and at no time perhaps more necessary than at the present.

The fourth resolution stands as follows:—

That the General Assembly doth also express its deep regret, that a spirit has in sundry instances, been manifested by the Federal Government, to enlarge its powers by forced constructions of the Constitutional charter which defines them; and that indications have appeared of a design to expound cer-

tain general phrases, (which, having been copied from the very limited grant of powers in the former articles of confederation were the less liable to be misconstrued) so as to destroy the meaning and effect, of the particular enumeration which necessarily explains, and limits the general phrases; and so as to consolidate the States by degrees, into one sovereignty, the obvious tendency and inevitable result of which would be, to transform the present republican system of the United States, into an absolute, or at best a mixed monarchy.

The *first* question here to be considered is, whether a spirit has in sundry instances been manifested by the Federal government to enlarge its powers by forced constructions of the constitutional charter.

The General Assembly having declared their opinion merely by regretting in general terms that forced constructions for enlarging the Federal powers have taken place, it does not appear to the committee necessary to go into a specification of every instance to which the resolution may allude. The Alien and Sedition Acts being particularly named in a succeeding resolution are of course to be understood as included in the allusion. Omitting others which have less occupied public attention, or been less extensively regarded as unconstitutional, the resolution may be presumed to refer particularly to the bank law, which from the circumstances of its passage as well as the latitude of construction on which it is founded, strikes the attention with singular force; and the carriage tax, distinguished also by circumstances in its history having a similar tendency. Those instances alone, if resulting from forced construction and calculated to enlarge the powers of the Federal government, as the committee cannot but conceive to be the case, sufficiently warrant this part of the resolution. The committee have not thought it incumbent on them to extend their attention to laws which have been objected to, rather as varying the constitutional distribution of powers in the Federal government, than as an absolute enlargement of them; because instances of this sort however important in their principles and tendencies, do not appear to fall strictly within the text under review.

The other questions presenting themselves, are—1. Whether indications have appeared of a design to expound certain general phrases copied from the "articles of confederation," so as to destroy the effect of the particular enumeration explaining and limiting their meaning. 2. Whether this exposition would by degrees consolidate the States into one sovereignty. 3. Whether the tendency and result of this consolidation would be to transform the republican system of the United States into a monarchy.

1. The general phrases here meant must be those "of providing for the common defence and general welfare."

In the "articles of confederation" the phrases are used as follows, in article VIII. "All charges of war, and all other expences that shall be incurred *for the common defence and general welfare*, and allowed by the United States in Congress assembled, shall be defrayed out of a common treasury, which shall be supplied by the several States, in proportion to the value of all land within each State, granted to or surveyed for any person, as such land and the buildings and improvements thereon shall be estimated, according to such mode as the United States in Congress assembled, shall from time to time direct and appoint."

In the existing Constitution, they make the following part of section 8. "The Congress shall have power, to lay and collect taxes, duties, imposts and excises to pay the debts, and provide for the common defence and general welfare of the United States."

This similarity in the use of these phrases in the two great federal charters, might well be considered, as rendering their meaning less liable to be misconstrued in the latter; because it will scarcely be said that in the former they were ever understood to be either a general grant of power, or to authorize the requisition or application of money by the old Congress to the common defence and general welfare, except in the cases afterwards enumerated which explained and limited their meaning; and if such was the limited meaning attached to these phrases in the very instrument revised and remodeled by the present Constitution, it can never be supposed that when copied into this Constitution, a different meaning ought to be attached to them.

That notwithstanding this remarkable security against misconstruction, a design has been indicated to expound these phrases in the Constitution so as to destroy the effect of the particular enumeration of powers by which it explains and limits them, must have fallen under the observation of those who have attended to the course of public transactions. Not to multiply proofs on this subject, it will suffice to refer to the debates of the Federal Legislature in which arguments have on different occasions been drawn, with apparent effect from these phrases in their indefinite meaning.

To these indications might be added without looking farther, the official report on manufactures by the late Secretary of the Treasury, made on the 5th of December, 1791; and the report of a committee of Congress in January, 1797, on the promotion of agriculture. In the first of these it is expressly contended to belong "to the discretion of the National "legislature to pronounce upon the objects which concern "the *general welfare,* and for which under that description, "an appropriation of money is requisite and proper. And there "seems to be no room for a doubt that whatever concerns the

"general interests of LEARNING, of AGRICULTURE, of MANUFAC-
"TURES, and of COMMERCE, are within the sphere of the na-
"tional councils, *as far as regards an application of money.*"
The latter report assumes the same latitude of power in the
national councils and applies it to the encouragement of agriculture, by means of a society to be established at the seat of
government. Although neither of these reports may have received the sanction of a law carrying it into effect; yet, on the
other hand, the extraordinary doctrine contained in both, has
passed without the slightest positive mark of disapprobation
from the authority to which it was addressed.

Now whether the phrases in question be construed to authorize every measure relating to the common defence and
general welfare, as contended by some; or every measure only
in which there might be an application of money, as suggested
by the caution of others, the effect must substantially be the
same, in destroying the import and force of the particular
enumeration of powers, which follow these general phrases in
the Constitution. For it is evident that there is not a single
power whatever, which may not have some reference to the
common defence, or the general welfare; nor a power of any
magnitude which in its exercise does not involve or admit
an application of money. The government therefore which
possesses power in either one or other of these extents, is a
government without the limitations formed by a particular
enumeration of powers; and consequently the meaning and
effect of this particular enumeration, is destroyed by the exposition given to these general phrases.

This conclusion will not be affected by an attempt to qual-
ify the power over the "general welfare," by referring it to
cases where the *general welfare* is beyond the reach of *separate* provisions by the *individual States;* and leaving to these
their jurisdictions in cases, to which their separate provisions

may be competent. For as the authority of the individual States must in all cases be incompetent to general regulations operating through the whole, the authority of the United States would be extended to every object relating to the general welfare, which might by any possibility be provided for by the general authority. This qualifying construction therefore would have little, if any tendency, to circumscribe the power claimed under the latitude of the terms "general welfare."

The true and fair construction of this expression, both in the original and existing Federal compacts appears to the committee too obvious to be mistaken. In both, the Congress is authorized to provide money for the common defence and *general welfare*. In both, is subjoined to this authority, an enumeration of the cases, to which their powers shall extend. Money cannot be applied to the *general welfare*, otherwise than by an application of it to some *particular* measure conducive to the general welfare. Whenever therefore, money has been raised by the general authority, and is to be applied to a particular measure, a question arises, whether the particular measure be within the enumerated authorities vested in Congress. If it be, the money requisite for it may be applied to it; if it be not, no such application can be made. This fair and obvious interpretation coincides with, and is enforced by, the clause in the Constitution which declares that "no money shall be drawn from the treasury, but in consequence of appropriations by law." An appropriation of money to the general welfare, would be deemed rather a mockery than an observance of this constitutional injunction.

2. Whether the exposition of the general phrases here combated, would not, by degrees consolidate the States into one sovereignty, is a question concerning which, the committee can perceive little room for difference of opinion. To consoli-

date the States into one sovereignty, nothing more can be wanted, than to supercede their respective sovereignties in the cases reserved to them, by extending the sovereignty of the United States to all cases of the "general welfare," that is to say, to *all cases whatever*.

3. That the obvious tendency and inevitable result of a consolidation of the States into one sovereignty, would be, to transform the republican system of the United States into a monarchy, is a point which seems to have been sufficiently decided by the general sentiment of America. In almost every instance of discussion, relating to the consolidation in question, its certain tendency to pave the way to monarchy, seems not to have been contested. The prospect of such a consolidation has formed the only topic of controversy. It would be unnecessary therefore, for the committee to dwell long on the reasons which support the position of the General Assembly. It may not be improper however to remark two consequences evidently flowing from an extension of the Federal powers to every subject falling within the idea of the "general welfare."

One consequence must be, to enlarge the sphere of discretion allotted to the executive magistrate. Even within the legislative limits properly defined by the Constitution, the difficulty of accomodating legal regulations to a country so great in extent, and so various in its circumstances, has been much felt; and has led to occasional investments of power in the executive, which involve perhaps as large a portion of discretion, as can be deemed consistent with the nature of the executive trust. In proportion as the objects of legislative care might be multiplied, would the time allowed for each be diminished, and the difficulty of providing uniform and particular regulations for all, be increased. From these sources would necessarily ensue, a greater latitude to the agency of that department which is always in existence, and which could best mould regulations of a general nature, so as to suit them to the diversity of particular situations. And it is in this latitude, as a supplement to the deficiency of the laws, that the degree of executive prerogative materially consists.

The other consequence would be, that of an excessive augmentation of the offices, honors, and emoluments depending on the executive will. Add to the present legitimate stock, all those of every description which a consolidation of the States would take from them, and turn over to the federal government, and the patronage of the executive would necessarily be as much swelled in this case, as its prerogative would be in the other.

This disproportionate increase of prerogative and patronage must, evidently, either enable the chief magistrate of the union, by quiet means, to secure his re-election from time to time, and finally, to regulate the succession as he might please; or, by giving so transcendent an importance to the office, would render the elections to it so violent and corrupt, that the public voice itself might call for an hereditary, in place of an elective succession. Which ever of these events might follow, the transformation of the Republican system of the United States into a monarchy, anticipated by the General Assembly from a consolidation of the States into one sovereignty, would be equally accomplished; and whether it would be into a mixt or an absolute monarchy, might depend on too many contingencies to admit of any certain foresight.

The resolution next in order, is contained in the following terms:

That the General Assembly doth particularly protest against the palpable, and alarming infractions of the Constitution, in the two late cases of the "Alien and Sedition acts," passed at the last session of Congress; the first of which, exercises a power no where delegated to the Federal government; and which by uniting legislative and judicial powers to those of executive, subverts the general principles of a free government, as well as the particular organization, and positive provisions of the Federal Constitution; and the other of which acts, exercises in like manner, a power not delegated by the Constitution, but on the contrary, expressly and positively forbidden by one of the amendments thereto;—a power, which more than any other, ought to produce universal alarm; because it is leveled against that right of freely examining public characters and measures, and of free communication among the people thereon, which has ever been justly deemed the only effectual guardian of every other right.

The subject of this resolution having, it is presumed, more particularly led the General Assembly into the proceedings which they communicated to the other States, and being in itself of peculiar importance; it deserves the most critical and faithful investigation; for the length of which no other apology will be necessary.

The subject divides itself into *first*, "The Alien Act," *secondly*, "The Sedition Act."

Of the "Alien Act," it is affirmed by the resolution, 1st. That it exercises a power no where delegated to the federal government. 2d. That it unites legislative and judicial powers to those of the executive. 3d. That this union of power, subverts the general principles of free government. 4th. That it subverts the particular organization and positive provisions of the Federal Constitution.

In order to clear the way for a correct view of the first position, several observations will be premised.

In the first place, it is to be borne in mind, that it being a characteristic feature of the Federal Constitution, as it was originally ratified, and an amendment thereto having precisely declared, "That the powers not delegated to the United States by the Constitution, nor prohibited by it to the States, are reserved to the States respectively, or to the people;" it is incumbent in this, as in every other exercise of power by the Federal government, to prove from the Constitution, that it grants the particular power exercised.

The next observation to be made, is, that much confusion and fallacy have been thrown into the question, by blending the two cases of *aliens, members of a hostile nation;* and *aliens, members of friendly nations.* These two cases are so obviously, and so essentially distinct, that it occasions no little surprise that the distinction should have been disregarded: and the surprise is so much the greater, as it appears that the two cases are actually distinguished by two separate acts of Congress, passed at the same session, and comprised in the same publication; the one providing for the case of "alien enemies;" the other "concerning aliens" indiscriminately; and consequently extending to aliens of every nation in peace and amity with the United States. With respect to alien enemies, no doubt has been intimated as to the federal authority over them; the Constitution having expressly delegated to Congress the power to declare war against any nation, and of course to treat it and all its members as enemies. With respect to aliens, who are not enemies, but members of nations in peace and amity with the United States, the power assumed by the act of Congress, is denied to be constitutional; and it is accordingly against this act, that the protest of the General Assembly is expressly and exclusively directed.

A third observation is, that were it admitted as is contended, that the "act concerning aliens," has for its object, not a *penal,* but a *preventive* justice; it would still remain to be proved that it comes within the constitutional power of the Federal legislature, and if within its power, that the legislature has exercised it in a constitutional manner.

In the administration of preventive justice, the following principles have been held sacred; that some probable ground of suspicion be exhibited before some judicial authority; that it be supported by oath or affirmation; that the party may avoid being thrown into confinement, by finding pledges or sureties for his legal conduct sufficient in the judgment of some judicial authority; that he may have the benefit of a writ of habeas corpus, and thus obtain his release, if wrongfully confined; and that he may at any time be discharged from his recognizance, or his confinement, and restored to his former liberty and rights, on the order of the proper judicial authority; if it shall see sufficient cause.

All these principles of the only preventive justice known to American jurisprudence, are violated by the Alien Act. The ground of suspicion is to be judged of, not by any judicial authority, but by the executive magistrate alone; no oath or affirmation is required; if the suspicion be held reasonable by the President, he may order the suspected alien to depart the territory of the United States, without the opportunity of avoiding the sentence, by finding pledges for his future good conduct; as the President may limit the time of departure as he pleases, the benefit of the writ of habeas corpus, may be suspended with respect to the party, although the Constitution ordains, that it shall not be suspended, unless when the public safety may require it in case of rebellion or invasion, neither of which existed at the passage of the act: And the party being, under the sentence of the President, either removed from the United States, or being punished by imprisonment, or disqualification ever to become a citizen on conviction of not obeying the order of removal, he cannot be discharged from the proceedings against him, and restored to the benefits of his former situation, although the *highest judicial authority* should see the most sufficient cause for it.

But, in the last place, it can never be admitted, that the removal of aliens, authorized by the act, is to be considered, not as punishment for an offence; but as a measure of precaution and prevention. If the banishment of an alien from a country into which he has been invited, as the asylum most auspicious to his happiness; a country, where he may have formed the most tender of connections, where he may have vested his entire property, and acquired property of the real and permanent, as well as the moveable and temporary kind; where he enjoys under the laws, a greater share of the blessings of personal security and personal liberty, than he can elsewhere hope for, and where he may have nearly compleated his probationary title to citizenship; if moreover, in the execution of the sentence against him, he is to be exposed, not only to the ordinary dangers of the sea, but to the peculiar casualties incident to a crisis of war, and of unusual licentiousness on that element, and possibly to vindictive purposes which his emigration itself may have provoked; if a banishment of this sort be not a punishment, and among the severest of punishments, it will be difficult to imagine a doom to which the name can be applied. And if it be a punishment, it will remain to be enquired, whether it can be constitutionally inflicted, on mere suspicion, by the single will of the executive magistrate, on persons convicted of no personal offence against the laws of the land, nor involved in any offence against the law of nations, charged on the foreign state of which they are members.

One argument offered in justification of this power exercised over aliens, is, that the admission of them into the country being of favor not of right, the favor is at all times revokable.

To this argument it might be answered, that allowing the truth of the inference, it would be no proof of what is required. A question would still occur, whether the Constitution had vested the discretionary power of admitting aliens in the federal government or in the State governments.

But it can not be a true inference, that because the admission of an alien is a favor, the favor may be revoked at pleasure. A grant of land to an individual, may be of favor not of right; but the moment the grant is made, the favor becomes a right, and must be forfeited before it can be taken away. To pardon a malefactor may be a favor, but the pardon is not, on that account, the less irrevocable. To admit an alien to naturalization, is as much a favor, as to admit him to reside in the country; yet it cannot be pretended, that a person naturalized can be deprived of the benefit, any more than a native citizen can be disfranchised.

Again it is said, that aliens not being parties to the Constitution, the rights and privileges which it secures, cannot be at all claimed by them.

To this reasoning also, it might be answered, that although aliens are not parties to the Constitution, it does not follow that the Constitution has vested in Congress an absolute power over them. The parties to the Constitution may have granted, or retained, or modified the power over aliens, without regard to that particular consideration.

But a more direct reply is, that it does not follow, because aliens are not parties to the Constitution, as citizens are parties to it, that whilst they actually conform to it, they have no right to its protection. Aliens are not more parties to the laws, than they are parties to the Constitution; yet it will not be disputed, that as they owe on one hand, a temporary obedience, they are entitled in return, to their protection and advantage.

If aliens had no rights under the constitution, they might not only be banished, but even capitally punished, without a jury or the other incidents to a fair trial. But so far has a contrary principle been carried, in every part of the United States, that except on charges of treason, an alien has, besides all the common privileges, the special one of being tried by a jury, of which one half may be also aliens.

It is said, further, that by the law and practice of nations, aliens may be removed at discretion, for offences against the law of nations; that Congress are authorized to define and punish such offences; and that to be dangerous to the peace of society is, in aliens, one of those offences.

The distinction between alien enemies and alien friends, is a clear and conclusive answer to this argument. Alien enemies are under the law of nations, and liable to be punished for offences against it. Alien friends, except in the single case of public ministers, are under the municipal law, and must be tried and punished according to that law only.

This argument also, by referring the Alien Act, to the power of Congress to define and *punish* offences against the law of nations, yields the point that the act is of a *penal*, not merely of a preventive operation. It must, in truth be so considered. And if it be a penal act, the punishment it inflicts, must be justified by some offence that deserves it.

Offenses for which aliens within the jurisdiction of a country, are punishable, are first, offences committed by the nation of which they make a part, and in whose offences they are involved: Secondly, offences committed by themselves alone, without any charge against the nation to which they belong. The first is the case of alien enemies; the second the case of alien friends. In the first case, the offending nation can no otherwise be punished than by war, one of the laws which authorizes the expulsion of such of its members, as may be found within the country, against which the offence has been committed. In the second case, the offence being committed by the individual, not by his nation, and against the municipal law, not against the law of nations; the individual only, and not the nation is punishable; and the punishment must be conducted according to the municipal law, not according to the law of nations. Under this view of the subject, the act of Congress, for the removal of alien enemies, being conformable to the law of nations, is justified by the Constitution: and the act, for the removal of alien friends, being repugnant to the constitutional principles of municipal law, is unjustifiable.

Nor is the act of Congress, for the removal of alien friends, more agreeable to the general practice of nations, than it is within the purview of the law of nations. The general practice of nations, distinguishes between alien friends and alien enemies. The latter it has proceeded against, according to the law of nations, by expelling them as enemies. The former it has considered as under a local and temporary allegiance, and entitled to a correspondent protection. If contrary instances are to be found in barbarous countries, under undefined prerogatives, or amid revolutionary dangers; they will not be deemed fit precedents for the government of the United States, even, if not beyond its constitutional authority.

It is said, that Congress may grant letters of marque and reprisal; that reprisals may be made on persons, as well as property; and that the removal of aliens may be considered as the exercise in an inferior degree, of the general power of reprisal on persons.

Without entering minutely into a question that does not seem to require it; it may be remarked, that reprisal is a seizure of foreign persons or property, with a view to obtain that justice for injuries done by one state or its members, to another state or its members; for which a refusal of the aggressor requires such a resort to force under the law of nations. It must be considered as an abuse of words to call the removal of persons from a country, a seizure or reprisal on them; nor is the distinction to be overlooked between reprisals on persons within the country and under the faith of its laws, and on persons out of the country. But, laying aside these considerations; it is evidently impossible to bring the Alien Act within the power of granting reprisals; since it does not allege or imply any injury received from any particular nation, for which this proceeding against its members was intended as a reparation. The proceeding is authorized against aliens *of every nation*; of nations charged neither with any similar proceeding against American citizens, nor with any injuries for which justice might be sought, in the mode prescribed by the act. Were it true therefore, that good causes existed for reprisals against one or more foreign nations, and that neither the persons nor property of its members under the faith of our laws, could plead an exemption; the operation of the act ought to have been limited to the aliens among us, belonging to such nations. To license reprisals against all nations, for aggressions charged on one only, would be a measure as contrary to every principle of justice and public law, as to a wise policy, and the universal practice of nations.

It is said, that the right of removing aliens is an incident to the power of war, vested in Congress by the Constitution.

This is a former argument in a new shape only; and is answered by repeating, that the removal of alien enemies is an incident to the power of war; that the removal of alien friends, is not an incident to the power of war.

It is said, that Congress, is, by the Constitution, to protect each State against invasion; and that the means of *preventing* invasion, are included in the power of protection against it.

The power of war in general, having been before granted by the Constitution, this clause must either be a mere specification for greater caution and certainty, of which there are other examples in the instrument; or be the injunction of a duty, superadded to a grant of the power. Under either explanation, it cannot enlarge the powers of Congress on the subject. The power and the duty to protect each state against an invading enemy, would be the same under the general power, if this regard to greater caution had been omitted.

Invasion is an operation of war. To protect against invasion is an exercise of the power of war. A power therefore not incident to war, cannot be incident to a particular modification of war. And as the removal of alien friends has appeared to be no incident to a general state of war, it cannot be incident to a partial state, or a particular modification of war.

Nor can it ever be granted, that a power to act on a case when it actually occurs, includes a power over all the means that may *tend to prevent* the occurrence of the case. Such a latitude of construction would render unavailing, every practicable definition of particular and limited powers. Under the idea of preventing war in general, as well as invasion in particular, not only an indiscriminate removal of all aliens, might be enforced; but a thousand other things still more remote from the operations and precautions appurtenant to war, might take place. A bigoted or tyrannical nation might threaten us with war, unless certain religious or political regulations were adopted by us; yet it never could be inferred, if the regulations which would prevent war, were such as Congress had otherwise no power to make, that the power to make them would grow out of the purpose they were to answer. Congress have power to suppress insurrections, yet it would not be allowed to follow, that they might employ all the means tending to prevent them; of which a system of moral instruction for the ignorant, and of provident support for the poor, might be regarded as among the most efficacious.

One argument for the power of the General Government to remove aliens would have been passed in silence, if it had appeared under any authority inferior to that of a report, made during the last session of Congress, to the House of Representatives by a committee, and approved by the House. The doctrine on which this argument is founded, is of so new and so extraordinary a character, and strikes so radically at the political system of America, that it is proper to state it in the very words of the report.

"The act [concerning aliens] is said to be unconstitutional, "because to remove aliens, is a direct breach of the Consti- "tution which provides, by the 9th section of the 1st article: "that the migration or importation of such persons as any of "the states shall think proper to admit, shall not be prohibited "by the Congress, prior to the year 1808."

Among the answers given to this objection to the constitutionality of the act, the following very remarkable one is extracted.

"Thirdly, that as the Constitution has *given to the States,* "no power to remove aliens, during the period of the limita- "tion under consideration, in the meantime, on the construc- "tion assumed, there would be no authority in the country, "empowered to send away dangerous aliens which cannot be "admitted."

The reasoning here used, would not in any view, be conclusive; because there are powers exercised by most other governments, which, in the United States are withheld by the people, both from the general government and from the State governments. Of this sort are many of the powers prohibited by the Declarations of right prefixed to the Constitutions, or by the clauses in the Constitutions, in the nature of such Declarations. Nay, so far is the political system of the United States distinguishable from that of other countries, by the caution with which powers are delegated and defined; that in one very important case, even of commercial regulation and revenue, the power is absolutely locked up against the hands of both governments. A tax on exports can be laid by no constitutional authority whatever. Under a system thus peculiarly guarded, there could surely be no absurdity in supposing, that alien friends, who if guilty of treasonable machinations may be punished, or if suspected on probable grounds, may be secured by pledges or imprisonment, in like manner with permanent citizens, were never meant to be subjected to banishment by any arbitrary and unusual process, either under the one government or the other.

But it is not the inconclusiveness of the general reasoning in this passage, which chiefly calls the attention to it. It is the principle assumed by it, that the powers held by the States, are given to them by the Constitution of the United States; and the inference from this principle, that the powers supposed to be necessary which are not so given to the State governments, must reside in the government of the United States.

The respect which is felt for every portion of the constituted authorities, forbids some of the reflections which this singular paragraph might excite; and they are the more readily suppressed, as it may be presumed, with justice perhaps, as well as candour, that inadvertence may have had its share in the error. It would be an unjustifiable delicacy nevertheless, to pass by so portentous a claim, proceeding from so high an authority, without a monitory notice of the fatal tendencies with which it would be pregnant.

Lastly, it is said, that a law on the same subject with the Alien Act, passed by this State originally in 1785, and re-enacted in 1792, is a proof that a summary removal of suspected aliens, was not heretofore regarded by the Virginia Legislature as liable to the objections now urged against such a measure.

This charge against Virginia, vanishes before the simple remark, that the law of Virginia relates to "suspicious persons, "being the subjects of any foreign power or state, who shall "have *made a declaration of war*, or actually *commenced hos-* "*tilities*, or from whom the President shall apprehend *hostile* "*designs;*" whereas the act of Congress relates to aliens, being the subjects of foreign powers and states, who have *neither declared war, nor commenced hostilities, nor from whom hostile designs are apprehended.*

II. It is next affirmed of the Alien Act, that it unites legislative, judicial and executive powers in the hands of the President.

However difficult it may be to mark, in every case, with clearness and certainty, the line which divides legislative power, from the other departments of power; all will agree, that the powers referred to these departments may be so general and undefined, as to be of a legislative, not of an executive or judicial nature; and may for that reason be unconstitutional. Details, to a certain degree, are essential to the nature and character of a law; and, on criminal subjects, it is proper, that details should leave as little as possible to the discretion of those who are to apply and to execute the law. If nothing more were required, in exercising a legislative trust, than a general conveyance of authority, without laying down any precise rules, by which the authority conveyed, should be carried into effect; it would follow, that the whole power of legislation might be transferred by the legislature from itself, and proclamations might become substitutes for laws. A delegation of power in this latitude, would not be denied to be a union of the different powers.

To determine then, whether the appropriate powers of the distinct departments are united by the act authorizing the executive to remove aliens, it must be enquired whether it contains such details, definitions, and rules, as appertain to the true character of a law; especially, a law by which personal liberty is invaded, property deprived of its value to the owner, and life itself indirectly exposed to danger.

The Alien Act, declares, "that it shall be lawful for the President to order all such aliens as he shall judge *dangerous* to the peace and safety of the United States, or shall have reasonable grounds to *suspect*, are concerned in any treasonable, *or secret machinations*, against the government thereof, to depart," &c.

Could a power be well given in terms less definite, less particular, and less precise? To be *dangerous to the public safety;* to be *suspected of secret machinations* against the government: these can never be mistaken for legal rules or certain definitions. They leave every thing to the President. His will is the law.

But it is not a legislative power only that is given to the President. He is to stand in the place of the judiciary also. His suspicion is the only evidence which is to convict: his order the only judgment which is to be executed.

Thus it is the President whose will is to designate the offensive conduct; it is his will that is to ascertain the individuals on whom it is charged; and it is his will, that is to cause the sentence to be executed. It is rightly affirmed therefore, that the act unites legislative and judicial powers to those of the executive.

III. It is affirmed that this union of powers subverts the general principles of free government.

It has become an axiom in the science of government, that a separation of the legislative, executive and judicial departments, is necessary to the preservation of public liberty. No where has this axiom been better understood in theory, or more carefully pursued in practice, than in the United States.

IV. It is affirmed that such a union of power subverts the particular organization and positive provisions of the Federal Constitution.

According to the particular organization of the Constitution, its legislative powers are vested in the Congress; its executive powers in the President, and its judicial powers, in a supreme and inferior tribunals. The union of any two of these powers, and still more of all three, in any one of these departments, as has been shewn to be done by the Alien Act, must consequently subvert the constitutional organization of them.

That positive provisions in the Constitution, securing to individuals the benefits of fair trial, are also violated by the union of powers in the Alien Act, necessarily results from the two facts, that the act relates to alien friends, and that alien friends being under the municipal law only, are entitled to its protection.

The *second* object against which the resolution protests is the Sedition Act.

Of this act it is affirmed 1. That it exercises in like manner a power not delegated by the Constitution. 2d. That the power, on the contrary, is expressly and positively forbidden by one of the amendments to the Constitution. 3d. That this is a power, which more than any other ought to produce universal alarm; because it is leveled against that right of freely examining public characters and measures, and of free communication thereon; which has ever been justly deemed the only effectual guardian of every other right.

I. That it exercises a power not delegated by the Constitution.

Here, again it will be proper to recollect, that the Federal

Government being composed of powers specifically granted, with a reservation of all others to the States or to the people, the positive authority under which the Sedition Act could be passed must be produced by those who assert its constitutionality. In what part of the Constitution then is this authority to be found?

Several attempts have been made to answer this question, which will be examined in their order. The committee will begin with one, which has filled them with equal astonishment and apprehension; and which, they cannot but persuade themselves, must have the same effect on all, who will consider it with coolness and impartiality, and with a reverence for our Constitution, in the true character in which it issued from the sovereign authority of the people. The committee refer to the doctrine lately advanced as a sanction to the Sedition Act: "that the common or unwritten law," a law of vast extent and complexity, and embracing almost every possible subject of legislation, both civil and criminal, "makes a part of the law of these States; in their united and national capacity."

The novelty, and in the judgment of the committee, the extravagance of this pretension, would have consigned it to the silence, in which they have passed by other arguments, which an extraordinary zeal for the act has drawn into the discussion. But the auspices, under which this innovation presents itself, have constrained the committee to bestow on it an attention, which other considerations might have forbidden.

In executing the task, it may be of use, to look back to the colonial state of this country, prior to the revolution; to trace the effect of the revolution which converted the colonies into independent States; to enquire into the import of the articles of confederation, the first instrument by which the union of the States was regularly established; and finally to consult the

Constitution of 1788, which is the oracle that must decide the important question.

In the State prior to the revolution, it is certain that the common law under different limitations, made a part of the colonial codes. But whether it be understood that the original colonists brought the law with them, or made it their law by adoption; it is equally certain that it was the separate law of each colony within its respective limits, and was unknown to them, as a law pervading and operating through the whole, as one society.

It could not possibly be otherwise. The common law was not the same in any two of the colonies; in some, the modifications were materially and extensively different. There was no common legislature, by which a common will, could be expressed in the form of a law; nor any common magistracy, by which such a law could be carried into practice. The will of each colony alone and separately, had its organs for these purposes.

This stage of our political history, furnishes no foothold for the patrons of this new doctrine.

Did then, the principle or operation of the great event which made the colonies, independent states, imply or introduce the common law, as a law of the union?

The fundamental principle of the revolution was, that the colonies were co-ordinate members with each other, and with Great Britain; of an Empire, united by a common Executive Sovereign, but not united by any common Legislative Sovereign. The Legislative power was maintained to be as complete in each American Parliament, as in the British Parliament. And the royal prerogative was in force in each colony, by virtue of its acknowledging the King for its Executive Magistrate, as it was in Great Britain, by virtue of a like acknowledgement there. A denial of these principles by Great Britain, and the assertion of them by America, produced the revolution.

There was a time indeed, when an exception to the Legislative separation of the several component and co-equal parts of the Empire, obtained a degree of acquiescence. The British Parliament was allowed to regulate the trade with foreign nations, and between the different parts of the Empire. This was however mere practice without right, and contrary to the true theory of the constitution. The conveniency of some regulations in both those cases, was apparent; and as there was no Legislature with power over the whole, nor any constitutional pre-eminence among the Legislatures of the several parts; it was natural for the Legislature of that particular part which was the eldest and the largest, to assume this function, and for the others to acquiesce in it. This tacit arrangement was the less criticised, as the regulations established by the British Parliament, operated in favor of that part of the Empire, which seemed to bear the principal share of the public burdens, and were regarded as an indemnification of its advances for the other parts. As long as this regulating power was confined to two objects of conveniency and equity, it was not complained of, nor much enquired into. But no sooner was it perverted to the selfish views of the party assuming it, than the injured parties began to feel and to reflect; and the moment the claim to a direct and indefinite power was ingrafted on the precedent of the regulating power, the whole charm was dissolved, and every eye opened to the usurpation. The assertion by G. B. of a power to make laws for the other members of the Empire *in all cases whatsoever*, ended in the discovery, that she had a right to make laws for them, *in no cases whatsoever*.

Such being the ground of our revolution, no support nor colour can be drawn from it, for the doctrine that the common law is binding on these States as one society. The doctrine on the contrary, is evidently repugnant to the fundamental principle of the revolution.

The articles of confederation, are the next source of information on this subject.

In the interval between the commencement of the revolution, and the final ratification of these articles, the nature and extent of the union was determined by the circumstances of the crisis, rather than by any accurate delineation of the general authority. It will not be alleged that the "common law," could have had any legitimate birth as a law of the United States, during that state of things. If it came as such, into existence at all, the charter of confederation must have been its parent.

Here again, however, its pretensions are absolutely destitute of foundation. This instrument does not contain a sentence or syllable, that can be tortured into a countenance of the idea, that the parties to it were with respect to the objects of the common law, to form one community. No such law is named or implied, or alluded to, as being in force, or as brought into force by that compact. No provision is made by which such a law could be carried into operation; whilst on the other hand, every such inference or pretext is abolutely precluded, by article 2d, which declares, "that each State retains its sovereignity, freedom and independence, and every power, jurisdiction and right, which is not by this confederation expressly delegated to the United States, in Congress assembled."

Thus far it appears, that not a vestige of this extraordinary doctrine can be found, in the origin or progress of American institutions. The evidence against it, has, on the contrary, grown stronger at every step; till it has amounted to a formal and positive exclusion, by written articles of compact among the parties concerned.

Is this exclusion revoked, and the common law introduced as a national law, by the present Constitution of the United States? This is the final question to be examined.

It is readily admitted, that particular parts of the common law, may have a sanction from the Constitution, so far as they are necessarily comprehended in the technical phrases which express the powers delegated to the government; and so far also, as such other parts may be adopted as necessary and proper, for carrying into execution the powers expressly delegated. But the question does not relate to either of these portions of the common law. It relates to the common law, beyond these limitations.

The only part of the Constitution which seems to have been relied on in this case, is the 2d sect. of art. III. The judicial power shall extend to all cases, *in law and equity*, arising *under this Constitution*, the "laws of the United States, and treaties made or which shall be made under their authority."

It has been asked what cases distinct from those arising under the laws and treaties of the United States, can arise under the Constitution, other than those arising under the common law; and it is inferred, that the common law is accordingly adopted or recognized by the Constitution.

Never perhaps was so broad a construction applied to a text so clearly unsusceptible of it. If any colour for the inference could be found, it must be in the impossibility of finding any other cases in law and equity, within the provision of the Constitution, to satisfy the expression; and rather than resort to a construction affecting so essentially the whole character of the government, it would perhaps be more rational to consider the expression as a mere pleonasm or inadvertence. But it is not necessary to decide on such a dilemma. The expression is fully satisfied, and its accuracy justified, by two descriptions of cases, to which the judicial authority is extended, and neither of which implies that the common law is the law of the United States. One of these descriptions comprehends the cases growing out of the restrictions on the legislative power of the States. For example, it is provided that "no State shall emit bills of credit," or "make any thing but gold and silver coin a tender in payment of debts." Should this prohibition be violated, and a suit *between citizens of the same State* be the consequence, this would be a case arising under the constitution before the judicial power of the United States. A second description comprehends suits between citizens and foreigners, or citizens of different States, to be decided according to the State or foreign laws; but submitted by the Constitution to the judicial power of the United States; the judicial power being, in several instances, extended beyond the legislative power of the United States.

To this explanation of the text, the following observations may be added.

The expression, cases in law and equity, is manifestly confined to cases of a civil nature; and would exclude cases of criminal jurisdiction. Criminal cases in law and equity, would be a language unknown to the law.

The succeeding paragraph of the same section, is in harmony with this construction. It is in these words—"In all cases affecting ambassadors, other public ministers and consuls, and those in which a State shall be party, the Supreme Court shall have original jurisdiction. *In all* the other cases [including cases in law and equity arising under the Constitution] the Supreme Court shall have *appellate* jurisdiction both as to law and *fact;* with such exceptions, and under such regulations as Congress shall make."

This paragraph, by expressly giving an *appellate* jurisdiction, in cases of law and equity arising under the Constitution, to *fact,* as well as to law, clearly excludes criminal cases, where the trial by jury is secured; because the fact, in such cases, is not a subject of appeal. And although the appeal is liable to such *exceptions* and regulations as Congress may adopt; yet it is not to be supposed that an exception of all criminal cases could be contemplated; as well because a discretion in Congress to make or omit the exception would be improper; as because it would have been unnecessary. The exception could as easily have been made by the Constitution itself, as referred to the Congress.

Once more, the amendment last added to the Constitution, deserves attention, as throwing light on this subject. "This judicial power of the United States shall not be construed to extend to any suit in law or equity, commenced or prosecuted against one of the United States, by citizens of another State, or by citizens or subjects of any foreign power." As it will not be pretended that any criminal proceeding could take place against a State, the terms *law* or *equity*, must be understood as appropriate to *civil* in exclusion of *criminal* cases.

From these considerations, it is evident, that this part of the Constitution, even if it could be applied at all, to the purpose for which it has been cited, would not include any cases whatever of a criminal nature; and consequently, would not authorise the inference from it, that the judicial authority extends to offences against the common law, as offences arising under the Constitution.

It is further to be considered, that even if this part of the Constitution could be strained into an application to every common law case, criminal as well as civil, it could have no effect in justifying the Sedition Act; which is an exercise of legislative, and not of judicial power: and it is the judicial power only of which the extent is defined in this part of the Constitution.

There are two passages in the Constitution, in which a description of the law of the United States, is found—The first is contained in article III. sect. 2, in the words following: "This Constitution, the laws of the United States, and treaties made, or which shall be made under their authority." The second is contained in the 2d paragraph of art. VI. as follows: "This Constitution and the laws of the United States which shall be made in pursuance thereof, and all treaties made, or which shall be made under the authority of the United States, shall be the supreme law of the land." The first of these descriptions was meant as a guide to the judges of the United States; the second as a guide to the judges in the several States. Both of them consist of an enumeration, which was evidently meant to be precise and compleat. If the common law had been understood to be a law of the United States, it is not possible to assign a satisfactory reason why it was not expressed in the enumeration.

In aid of these objections, the difficulties and confusion inseparable from a constructive introduction of the common law, would afford powerful reasons against it.

Is it to be the common law with, or without the British statutes?

If without the statutory amendments, the vices of the code would be insupportable?

If with these amendments, what period is to be fixed for limiting the British authority over our laws?

Is it to be the date of the eldest or the youngest of the colonies?

Or are the dates to be thrown together, and a medium deduced?

Or is our independence to be taken for the date?

Is, again, regard to be had to the various changes in the common law made by the local codes of America?

Is regard to be had to such changes, subsequent, as well as prior, to the establishment of the Constitution?

Is regard to be had to future, as well as past changes?

Is the law to be different in every State, as differently modified by its code; or are the modifications of any particular State, to be applied to all?

And on the latter supposition, which among the State codes would form the standard?

Questions of this sort might be multiplied with as much case, as there would be difficulty in answering them.

The consequences flowing from the proposed contruction, furnish other objections equally conclusive; unless the text were peremptory in its meaning, and consistent with other parts of the instrument.

These consequences may be in relation; to the legislative authority of the United States; to the executive authority; to the judicial authority, and to the governments of the several States.

If it be understood that the common law is established by the Constitution, it follows that no part of the law can be altered by the legislature; such of the statutes already passed as may be repugnant thereto, would be nullified, particularly the "Sedition Act" itself which boasts of being a melioration of the common law; and the whole code with all its incongruities, barbarisms, and bloody maxims would be inviolably saddled on the good people of the United States.

Should this consequence be rejected, and the common law be held, like other laws, liable to revision and alteration, by the authority of Congress; it then follows, that the authority of Congress is co-extensive with the objects of common law; that is to say, with every object of legislation: For to every such object, does some branch or other of the common law extend. The authority of Congress would therefore be no longer under the limitations, marked out in the Constitution. They would be authorized to legislate in all cases whatsoever.

In the next place, as the President possesses the executive powers of the Constitution, and is to see that the laws be faithfully executed, his authority also must be co-extensive with every branch of the common law. The additions which this would make to his power, though not readily to be estimated, claims the most serious attention.

This is not all; it will merit the most profound consideration, how far an indefinite admission of the common law, with a latitude in construing it, equal to the construction by which it is deduced from the Constitution, might draw after it the various prerogatives making part of the unwritten law of England. The English constitution itself is nothing more than a composition of unwritten laws and maxims.

In the third place, whether the common law be admitted as of legal or of constitutional obligation, it would confer on the judicial department a discretion little short of a legislative power.

On the supposition of its having a constitutional obligation, this power in the judges would be permanent and irremediable by the legislature. On the other supposition, the power would not expire, until the legislature should have introduced a full system of statutory provisions. Let it be observed too, that besides all the uncertainties above enumerated, and which present an immense field for judicial discretion, it would remain with the same department to decide what parts of the common law would, and what would not, be properly applicable to the circumstances of the United States.

A discretion of this sort, has always been lamented as incongruous and dangerous, even in the colonial and State courts; although so much narrowed by positive provisions in the local codes on all the principal subjects embraced by the common law. Under the United States, where so few laws exist on those subjects, and where so great a lapse of time must happen before the vast chasm could be supplied, it is manifest that the power of the judges over the law would, in fact, erect them into legislators; and that for a long time, it would be impossible for the citizens to conjecture, either what was, or would be law.

In the last place, the consequence of admitting the common law as the law of the United States, on the authority of the individual States, is as obvious as it would be fatal. As this law relates to every subject of legislation, and would be paramount to the constitutions and laws of the States, the admission of it would overwhelm the residuary sovereignty of the States, and by one constructive operation new model the whole political fabric of the country.

From the review thus taken of the situation of the American colonies prior to their independence; of the effect of this event on their situation; of the nature and import of the articles of confederation; of the true meaning of the passage in the existing Constitution from which the common law has been deduced; of the difficulties and uncertainties incident to the doctrine; and of its vast consequences in extending the powers of the federal government, and in superceding the authorities of the State governments; the committee feel the utmost confidence in concluding that the common law never was, nor by any fair construction, ever can be, deemed a law for the American people as one community; and they indulge the strongest expectation that the same conclusion will finally be drawn, by all candid and accurate enquirers into the subject. It is indeed distressing to reflect, that it ever should have been made a question, whether the Constitution, on the whole face of which is seen so much labour to enumerate and define the several objects of federal power, could intend to introduce in the lump, in an indirect manner, and by a forced construction of a few phrases, the vast and multifarious jurisdiction involved in the common law; a law filling so many ample volumes; a law overspreading the entire field of legislation; and a law that would sap the foundation of the Constitution as a system of limited and specified powers. A severer reproach could not in the opinion of the committee be thrown on the Constitution, on those who framed, or on those who established it, than such a supposition would throw on them.

The argument then drawn from the common law, on the ground of its being adopted or recognized by the Constitution, being inapplicable to the Sedition Act, the committee will proceed to examine the other arguments which have been founded on the Constitution.

They will waste but little time on the attempt to cover the act by the preamble to the Constitution; it being contrary to every acknowledged rule of construction, to set up this part of an instrument, in opposition to the plain meaning, expressed in the body of the instrument. A preamble usually contains the general motives or reasons, for the particular regulations or measures which follow it; and is always understood to be explained and limited by them. In the present instance, a contrary interpretation would have the inadmissable effect, of rendering nugatory or improper, every part of the Constitution which succeeded the preamble.

The paragraph in art. 1, sect. 8, which contains the power to lay and collect taxes, duties, imposts, and excises, to pay the debts, and provide for the common defence and general welfare, having been already examined, will also require no particular attention in this place. It will have been seen that in its fair and consistent meaning, it cannot enlarge the enumerated powers vested in Congress.

The part of the Constitution which seems most to be recurred to, in defence of the "Sedition Act," is the last clause of the above section, empowering Congress "to make all laws which shall be necessary and proper for carrying into execution the foregoing powers, and all other powers vested by this Constitution in the government of the United States, or in any department or officer thereof."

The plain import of this clause is, that Congress shall have all the incidental or instrumental powers, necessary and proper for carrying into execution all the express powers; whether they be vested in the government of the United States, more collectively, or in the several departments, or officers thereof. It is not a grant of new powers to Congress, but merely a declaration, for the removal of all uncertainty, that the means of carrying into execution, those otherwise granted, are included in the grant.

Whenever, therefore a question arises concerning the constitutionality of a particular power; the first question is, whether the power be expressed in the Constitution. If it be, the question is decided. If it be not expressed; the next enquiry must be, whether it is properly an incident to an express power, and necessary to its execution. If it be, it may be exercised by Congress. If it be not; Congress cannot exercise it.

Let the question be asked, then, whether the power over the press exercised in the "Sedition Act," be found among the powers expressly vested in the Congress? This is not pretended.

Is there any express power, for executing which, it is necessary and proper power?

The power which has been selected, as least remote, in answer to this question, is that of "suppressing insurrections;" which is said to imply a power to *prevent* insurrections, by punishing whatever may *lead* or *tend* to them. But it surely cannot, with the least plausibility, be said, that a regulation of the press, and a punishment of libels, are exercises of a power to suppress insurrections. The most that could be said, would be, that the punishment of libels, if it had the tendency ascribed to it, might prevent the occasion, of passing or executing laws, necessary and proper for the suppression of insurrections.

Has the federal government no power, then, to prevent as well as to punish resistance to the laws;

They have the power which the Constitution deemed most proper in their hands for the purpose. The Congress has power, before it happens, to pass laws for punishing it; and the Executive and Judiciary have power to enforce those laws when it does happen.

It must be recollected by many, and could be shewn to the satisfaction of all, that the construction here put on the terms "necessary and proper" is precisely the construction which prevailed during the discussions and ratifications of the Constitution. It may be added, and cannot too often be repeated, that it is a construction absolutely necessary to maintain their consistency with the peculiar character of the government, as possessed of particular and defined powers only; not of the general and indefinite powers vested in ordinary governments. For if the power to *suppress insurrections*, includes a power to *punish libels;* or if the power to *punish,* includes a power to *prevent,* by all the means that may have that *tendency;* such is the relation and influence among the most remote subjects of legislations, that a power over a very few, would carry with it a power over all. And it must be wholly immaterial, whether unlimited powers be exercised under the name of unlimited powers, or be exercised under the name of unlimited means of carrying into execution, limited powers.

This branch of the subject will be closed with a reflection which must have weight with all; but more especially with those who place peculiar reliance on the judicial exposition of the Constitution, as the bulwark provided against undue extensions of the legislative power. If it be understood that the powers implied in the specified powers, have an immediate and appropriate relation to them, as means, necessary and proper for carrying them into execution, questions on the constitutionality of laws passed for this purpose, will be of a nature sufficiently precise and determinate for judicial cognizance and control. If, on the other hand, Congress are not limited in the choice of means by any such appropriate relation of them to the specified powers; but may employ all such means as they may deem fitted to *prevent* as well as to *punish*, crimes subjected to their authority; such as may have a *tendency* only to *promote* an object for which they are authorized to provide; every one must perceive that questions relating to means of this sort, must be questions of mere policy and expediency; on which legislative discretion alone can decide, and from which the judicial interposition and controul are completely excluded.

II. The next point which the resolution requires to be proved, is, that the power over the press exercised by the Sedition Act, is positively forbidden by one of the amendments to the Constitution.

The amendment stands in these words—"Congress shall make no law respecting an establishment of religion, or prohibiting the free exercise thereof, *or abridging the freedom of speech or of the press*; or the right of the people peaceably to assemble, and to petition the government for a redress of grievances."

In the attempts to vindicate the "Sedition Act," it has been contended, 1. That the "freedom of the press" is to be determined by the meaning of these terms in the common law. 2. That the article supposes the power over the press to be in Congress, and prohibits them only from *abridging* the freedom allowed to it by the common law.

Although it will be shewn, in examining the second of these positions, that the amendment is a denial to Congress of all power over the press; it may not be useless to make the following observations on the first of them.

It is deemed to be a sound opinion, that the Sedition Act, in its definition of some of the crimes created, is an abridgment of the freedom of publication, recognized by principles of the common law in England.

The freedom of the press under the common law, is, in the defences of the Sedition Act, made to consist in an exemption from all *previous* restraint on printed publications, by persons authorized to inspect and prohibit them. It appears to the committee, that this idea of the freedom of the press, can never be admitted to be the American idea of it: since a law inflicting penalties on printed publications, would have a familiar effect with a law authorizing a previous restraint on them. It would seem a mockery to say, that no law should be passed, preventing publications from being made, but that laws might be passed for punishing them in case they should be made.

The essential difference between the British government, and the American Constitution, will place this subject in the clearest light.

In the British government, the danger of encroachments on the rights of the people, is understood to be confined to the executive magistrate. The representatives of the people in the legislature, are not only exempt themselves, from distrust, but are considered as sufficient guardians of the rights of their constituents against the danger from the executive. Hence it is a principle, that the parliament is unlimited in its powers; or in their own language, is omnipotent. Hence too, all the ramparts for protecting the rights of the people, such as their magna charta, their bill of rights, &c. are not reared against the parliament, but against the royal prerogative. They are merely legislative precautions, against executive usurpations. Under such a government as this, an exemption of the press from previous restraint by licensers appointed by the king, is all the freedom that can be secured to it.

In the United States, the case is altogether different. The people, not the government, possess the absolute sovereignty. The legislature, no less than the executive, is under limitations of power. Encroachments are regarded as possible from the one, as well as from the other. Hence in the United States, the great and essential rights of the people are secured against legislative, as well as against executive ambition. They are secured, not by laws paramount to prerogative; but by constitutions paramount to laws. This security of the freedom of the press, requires that it should be exempt, not only from previous restraint by the executive, as in Great Britain; but from legislative restraint also; and this exemption, to be effectual, must be an exemption, not only from the previous inspection of licensers, but from the subsequent penalty of laws.

The state of the press, therefore, under the common law, can not in this point of view, be the standard of its freedom in the United States.

But there is another view, under which it may be necessary to consider this subject. It may be alleged, that although the security for the freedom of the press, be different in Great Britain and in this country; being a legal security only in the former, and a constitutional security in the latter; and although there may be a further difference, in an extension of the freedom of the press, here, beyond an exemption from previous restraint, to an exemption from subsequent penalties also; yet that the actual legal freedom of the press, under the common law, must determine the degee of freedom, which is meant by the terms and which is constitutionally secured against both previous and subsequent restraints.

The committee are not aware of the difficulty of all general questions which, may turn on the proper boundary between the liberty and licentiousness of the press. They will leave it therefore for consideration only, how far the difference between the nature of the British government, and the nature of the American governments, and the practice under the latter, may shew the degree of rigor in the former, to be inapplicable to, and not obligatory in, the latter.

The nature of government elective, limited and responsible, in all their branches, may well be supposed to require a greater freedom of animadversion, than might be tolerated by the genuis of such a government as that of Great Britain. In the latter, it is a maxim, that the king, an hereditary, not a responsible magistrate, can do no wrong; and that the legislature, which in two thirds of its composition, is also hereditary, not responsible, can do what it pleases. In the United States, the executive magistrates are not held to be infallible, nor the legislatures to be omnipotent; and both being elective, are both responsible. Is it not natural and necessary, under such different circumstances, that a different degree of freedom, in the use of the press, should be contemplated?

Is not such an inference favored by what is observable in Great Britain itself? Notwithstanding the general doctrine of the common law, on the subject of the press, and the occasional punishment of those, who use it with a freedom offensive to the government; it is well known, that with respect to the responsible members of the government, where the reasons operating here, become applicable there; the freedom exercised by the press, and protected by the public opinion, far exceeds the limits prescribed by the ordinary rules of law. The ministry, who are responsible to impeachment, are at all times, animadverted on, by the press, with peculiar freedom; and during the elections for the House of Commons, the other responsible part of the government, the press is employed with as little reserve towards the candidates.

The practice in America must be entitled to much more respect. In every state, probably, in the union, the press has exerted a freedom in canvassing the merits and measures of public men, of every description, which has not been confined to the strict limits of the common law.—On this footing, the freedom of the press has stood; on this footing it yet stands. And it will not be a breach, either of truth or of candour, to say, that no persons or presses are in the habit of more unrestrained animadversions on the proceedings and functionaries of the State governments, than the persons and presses most zealous, in vindicating the act of Congress for punishing similar animadversions on the government of the United States.

The last remark will not be understood, as claiming for the State governments, an immunity greater than they have heretofore enjoyed. Some degree of abuse is inseparable from the proper use of every thing; and in no instance is this more true, than in that of the press. It has accordingly been decided by the practice of the States, that it is better to leave a few of its noxious branches, to their luxuriant growth, than by pruning them away, to injure the vigor of those yielding the proper fruits. And can the wisdom of this policy be doubted by any who reflect, that to the press alone, chequered as it is with abuses, the world is indebted for all the triumphs which have been gained by reason and humanity, over error and oppression; who reflect that to the same beneficient source, the United States owe much of the lights which conducted them to the rank of a free and independent nation; and which have improved their political system, into a shape so auspicious to their happiness. Had "sedition acts," fobidding every publication that might bring the constituted agents into contempt or disrepute, or that might excite the hatred of the people against the authors of unjust or pernicious measures, been uniformly enforced against the press; might not the United States have been languishing at this day, under the infirmities of a sickly confederation? Might they not possibly be miserable colonies, groaning under a foreign yoke?

To these observations one fact will be added, which demonstrates that the common law cannot be admitted as the *universal* expositor of American terms, which may be the same with those contained in that law. The freedom of conscience, and of religion, are found in the same instruments, which assert the freedom of the press. It will never be admitted, that the meaning of the former, in the common law of England, is to limit their meaning in the United States.

Whatever weight may be allowed to these considerations, the committee do not, however, by any means, intend to rest the question on them. They contend that the article of amendment, instead of supposing in Congress, a power that might be exercised over the press, provided its freedom be not abridged, was meant as a positive denial to Congress, of any power whatever on the subject.

To demonstrate that this was the true object of the article, it will be sufficient to recall the circumstances which led to it, and to refer to the explanation accompanying the article.

When the Constitution was under the discussions which preceded its ratification, it is well known, that great apprehensions were expressed by many, lest the omission of some positive exception from the powers delegated, of certain rights, and of the freedom of the press particularly, might expose them to the danger of being drawn by construction within some of the powers vested in Congress; more especially of the power to make all laws necessary and proper, for carrying their other powers into execution. In reply to this objection, it was invariably urged to be a fundamental and characteristic principle of the Constitution that all powers not given by it, were reserved; that no powers were given beyond those enumerated in the Constitution, and such as were fairly incident to them; that the power over the rights in question, and particularly over the press, was neither among the enumerated powers, nor incident to any of them; and consequently that an exercise of any such power, would be a manifest usurpation. It is painful to remark, how much the arguments now employed in behalf of the Sedition Act are at variance with the reasoning which then justified the Constitution, and invited its ratification.

From this posture of the subject, resulted the interesting question in so many of the conventions, whether the doubts and dangers ascribed to the Constitution should be removed by any amendments previous to the ratification, or be postponed, in confidence that as far as they might be proper, they would be introduced in the form provided by the Constitution. The latter course was adopted, and in most of the States, the ratifications were followed by propositions and instructions for rendering the Constitution more explicit, and more safe to the rights, not meant to be delegated by it. Among those rights, the freedom of the press, in most instances, is particularly and emphatically mentioned. The firm and very pointed manner, in which it is asserted in the proceedings of the convention of this State will be hereafter seen.

In pursuance of the wishes thus expressed, the first Congress that assembled under the constitution, proposed certain amendments which have since, by the necessary ratifications, been made a part of it; among which amendments is the article containing, among other prohibitions on the Congress, an express declaration that they should make no law abridging the freedom of the press.

Without tracing farther the evidence on this subject, it would seem scarcely possible to doubt, that no power whatever over the press, was supposed to be delegated by the Constitution, as it originally stood; and that the amendment was intended as a positive and absolute reservation of it.

But the evidence is still stronger. The proposition of amendments made by Congress, is introduced in the following terms: *"The Convention of a number of the States having at the time of their adopting the Constitution, expressed a desire, in order to prevent misconstructions or abuse of its powers, that further declaratory and restrictive clauses should be added; and as extending the ground of public confidence in the government, will best ensure the beneficent ends of its institutions."*

Here is the most satisfactory and authentic proof, that the several amendments proposed, were to be considered as either declaratory or restrictive; and whether the one or the other, as corresponding with the desire expressed by a number of the States, and as extending the ground of public confidence in the government.

Under any other construction of the amendment relating to the press, than that it declared the press to be wholly exempt from the power of Congress, the amendment could neither be said to correspond with the desire expressed by a number of the States, nor be calculated to extend the ground of public confidence in the government.

Nay more; the construction employed to justify the "Sedition Act," would exhibit a phenomenon, without a parallel in the political world. It would exhibit a number of respectable States, as denying first that any power over the press was delegated by the Constitution; as proposing next, that an amendment to it, should explicitly declare that no such power was delegated; and finally, as concurring in an amendment actually recognizing or delegating such a power.

Is then the Federal government, it will be asked, destitute of every authority for restraining the licentiousness of the press, and for shielding itself against the libellous attacks which may be made on those who administer it?

The Constitution alone can answer this question. If no such power be expressly delegated, and it be not both necessary and proper to carry into execution an express power; above all, if it be expressly forbidden by a declaratory amendment to the Constitution, the answer must be, that the Federal government is destitute of all such authority.

And might it not be asked in turn, whether it is not more probable, under all the circumstances which have been reviewed, that the authority should be withheld by the Constitution, than that it should be left to a vague and violent construction: whilst so much pains were bestowed in enumerating other powers, and so many less important powers are included in the enumeration.

Might it not be likewise asked, whether the anxious circumspection which dictated so many *peculiar* limitations on the general authority, would be unlikely to exempt the press altogether from that authority? The peculiar magnitude of some of the powers necessarily committed to the Federal government; the peculiar duration required for the functions of some of its departments; the peculiar distance of the seat of its proceedings from the great body of its constituents; and the peculiar difficulty of circulating an adequate knowledge of them through any other channel; will not these considerations, some or other of which produced other exceptions from the powers of ordinary governments, all together, account for the policy of binding the hand of the Federal government, from touching the channel which alone can give efficacy to its responsibility to its constituents; and of leaving those who administer it, to a remedy for injured reputations, under the same laws, and in the same tribunals, which protect their lives, their liberties, and their properties.

But the question does not turn either on the wisdom of the Constitution, or on the policy which gave rise to its particular organization. It turns on the actual meaning of the instrument; by which it has appeared, that a power over the press is clearly excluded, from the number of powers delegated to the Federal government.

III. And in the opinion of the committee well may it be said, as the resolution concludes with saying, that the unconstitutional power exercised over the press by the "Sedition Act," ought "more than anyother, to produce universal alarm; "because it is leveled against that right of freely examining "public characters and measures, and of free communication "among the people thereon, which has ever been justly deemed the only effectual guardian of every other right."

Without scrutinizing minutely into all the provisions of the "Sedition Act," it will be sufficient to cite so much of section 2. as follows: "And be it further enacted, that if any "person shall write, print, utter or publish, or shall cause or "procure to be written, printed, uttered or published, or shall "knowingly and willingly assist or aid in writing, printing, "uttering or publishing any false, scandalous, and malicious "writing or writings against the government of the United "States, or either house of the Congress of the United States, "or the President of the United States, *with an intent to de-* "*fame the said government, or either house of the said Con-* "*gress, or the President, or to bring them, or either of them,* "*into contempt or disrepute; or to excite against them, or ei-* "*ther, or any of them, the hatred of the good people of the* "*United States, &c. Then such person being thereof convicted* "*before any court of the United States, having jurisdiction*

"thereof, shall be punished by a fine not exceeding two thou-
"sand dollars, and by imprisonment not exceeding two years."

On this part of the act the following observations present themselves.

1. The Constitution supposes that the President, the Congress, and each of its houses, may not discharge their trusts, either from defect of judgment, or other causes. Hence, they are all made responsible to their constituents, at the returning periods of election; and the President, who is singly entrusted with very great powers, is, as a further guard, subjected to an intermediate impeachment.

2. Should it happen, as the Constitution supposes it may happen, that either of these branches of the government, may not have duly discharged its trust; it is natural and proper, that according to the cause and degree of their faults, they should be brought into contempt or disrepute, and incur the hatred of the people.

3. Whether it has, in any case, happened that the proceedings of either, or all of those branches, evinces such a violation of duty as to justify a contempt, a disrepute or hatred among the people, can only be determined by a free examination thereof, and a free communication among the people thereon.

4. Whenever it may have actually happened, that proceedings of this sort are chargeable on all or either of the branches of the government, it is the duty as well as right of intelligent and faithful citizens, to discuss and promulgate them freely, as well to controul them by the censorship of the public opinion, as to promote a remedy according to the rules of the Constitution. And it cannot be avoided, that those who are to apply the remedy must feel, in some degree, a contempt or hatred against the transgressing party.

5. As the act was passed on July 14, 1798, and is to be in force until March 3, 1801, it was of course, that during its

continuance, two elections of the entire House of Representatives, an election of a part of the Senate, and an election of a President, were to take place.

6. That consequently, during all these elections, intended by the Constitution to preserve the purity, or to purge the faults of the administration, the great remedial rights of the people were to be exercised, and the responsibility of their public agents to be screened, under the penalities of this act.

May it not be asked of every intelligent friend to the liberties of his country whether, the power exercised in such an act as this, ought not to produce great and universal alarm? Whether a rigid execution of such an act, in time past, would not have repressed that information and communication among the people, which is indispensable to the just exercise of their electoral rights? And whether such an act, if made perpetual, and enforced with rigor, would not, in time to come, either destroy our free system of government, or prepare a convulsion that might prove equally fatal to it.

In answer to such questions, it has been pleaded that the writings and publications forbidden by the act, are those only which are false and malicious, and intended to defame; and merit is claimed for the privilege allowed to authors to justify, by proving the truth of their publications, and for the limitations to which the sentence of fine and imprisonment is subjected.

To those who concurred in the act, under the extraordinary belief, that the option lay between the passing of such an act, and leaving in force the common law of libels, which punishes truth equally with falsehood, and submits the fine and imprisonment to the indefinite discretion of the court, the merit of good intentions ought surely not to be refused. A like merit may perhaps be due for the discontinuance of the *corporal punishment* which the common law also leaves to the discretion

70

of the court.—This merit of *intention*, however, would have been greater, if the several mitigations had not been limited to so short a period; and the apparent inconsistency would have been avoided, between justifying the act at one time, by contrasting it with the rigors of the common law, otherwise in force; and at another time by appealing to the nature of the crisis, as requiring the temporary rigor exerted by the act.

But whatever may have been the meritorious intentions of all or any who contributed to the Sedition Act, a very few reflections will prove, that its baneful tendency is little diminished by the privilege of giving in evidence the truth of the matter contained in political writings.

In the first place, where simple and naked facts alone are in question, there is sufficient difficulty in some cases, and sufficient trouble and vexation in all, of meeting a prosecution from the government, with the full and formal proof, necessary in a court of law.

But in the next place, it must be obvious to the plainest minds; that opinions, and inferences, and conjectural observations, are not only in many cases inseparable from the facts, but may often be more the objects of the prosecution than the facts themselves; or may even be altogether abstracted from particular facts; and that opinions and inferences, and conjectural observations, cannot be subjects of that kind of proof which appertains to facts, before a court of law.

Again, it is no less obvious, that the *intent* to defame or bring into contempt or disrepute, or hatred, which is made a condition of the offence created by the act; cannot prevent its pernicious influence, on the freedom of the press. For omitting the enquiry, how far the malice of the intent is an inference of the law from the mere publication; it is manifestly impossible to punish the intent to bring those who administer the government into disrepute or contempt, without striking at the right of freely discussing public characters and measures: because those who engage in such discussions, must expect and *intend* to excite these unfavorable sentiments, so far as they may be thought to be deserved. To prohibit therefore the intent to excite those unfavorable sentiments against those who administer the government, is equivalent to a prohibition of the actual excitement of them; and to prohibit the actual excitement of them, is equivalent to a prohibition of discussions having that tendency and effect; which, again, is equivalent to a protection of those who administer the government, if they should at any time deserve the contempt or hatred of the people, against being exposed to it, by free animadversions on their characters and conduct. Nor can there be a doubt, if those in public trust be shielded by penal laws from such strictures of the press, as may expose them to contempt or disrepute, or hatred, where they may deserve it, that in exact proportion as they may deserve to be exposed, will be the certainty and criminality of the intent to expose them, and the vigilance of prosecuting and punishing it; nor a doubt, that a government thus intrenched in penal statutes, against the just and natural effects of a culpable administration, will easily evade the responsibility, which is essential to a faithful discharge of its duty.

Let it be recollected, lastly, that the right of electing the members of the government, constitutes more particularly the essence of a free and responsible government. The value and efficacy of this right, depends on the knowledge of the comparative merits and demerits of the candidates for public trust; and on the equal freedom, consequently, of examining and discussing these merits and demerits of the candidates respectively. It has been seen that a number of important elections will take place whilst the act is in force; although it should not be continued beyond the term to which it is limited. Should there happen, then, as is extremely probable in relation to some or other of the branches of the government, to be competition between those who are, and those who are not, members of the government; what will be the situations of the competitors? Not equal; because the characters of the former will be covered by the "Sedition Act" from animadversions exposing them to disrepute among the people; whilst the latter may be exposed to the contempt and hatred of the people, without a violation of the act? What will be the situation of the people? Not free; because they will be compelled to make their election between competitors, whose pretensions they are not permitted by the act, equally to examine, to discuss, and to ascertain. And from both these situations, will not those in power derive an undue advantage for continuing themselves in it; which by impairing the right of election, endangers the blessings of the government founded on it.

It is with justice, therefore, that the General Assembly hath affirmed in the resolution, as well that the right of freely examining public characters and measures, and of free communication thereon, is the only effectual guardian of every other right; as that this particular right is leveled at, by the power exercised in the "Sedition Act."

The resolution next in order is as follows:

That this State having by its Convention, which ratified the Federal Constitution, expressly declared, that among other essential rights, "the liberty of conscience and of the press cannot be cancelled, abridged, restrained or modified by any authority of the United States," and from its extreme anxiety to guard these rights from every possible attack of sophistry and ambition, having with other States, recommended an amendment for that purpose, which amendment was, in due, time, annexed to the Constitution; it would mark a reproachful inconsistency, and criminal degeneracy, if an indifference were not shewn, to the most palpable violation of one of the rights, thus declared and secured; and to the establishment of a precedent, which may be fatal to the other.

To place this resolution in its just light, it will be necessary to recur to the act of ratification by Virginia which stands in the ensuing form.

We, the Delegates of the people of Virginia, duly elected in pursuance of a recommendation from the General Assembly, and now met in Convention, having fully and freely investigated and discussed the proceedings of the federal convention, and being prepared as well as the most mature deliberation hath enabled us, to decide thereon; DO, in the name and in behalf of the people of Virginia, declare and make known, that the powers granted under the Constitution, being derived from the people of the United States, may be resumed by them, whensoever the same shall be perverted to their injury or oppression; and that every power not granted thereby, remains with them, and at their will. That therefore, no right of any denomination can be cancelled, abridged, restrained or modified, by the Congress, by the Senate or House of Representatives acting in any capacity, by the President, or any department or officer of the United States, except in those instances in which power is given by the Constitution for those purposes; and, that among other essential rights, the liberty of conscience and of the press, cannot be cancelled, abridged, restrained or modified by any authority of the United States.

Here is an express and solemn declaration by the convention of the State, that they ratified the Constitution in the sense, that no right of any denomination can be cancelled, abridged, restrained or modified by the government of the United States or any part of it; except in those instances in which power is given by the Constitution; and in the sense particularly, "that among other essential rights, the liberty of conscience and freedom of the press cannot be cancelled, abridged, restrained or modified, by any authority of the United States."

Words could not well express, in a fuller or more forcible manner, the understanding of the convention, that the liberty of conscience and the freedom of the press, were *equally* and *completely* exempted from all authority whatever of the United States.

Under an anxiety to guard more effectually these rights against every possible danger, the convention, after ratifying the Constitution, proceeded to prefix to certain amendments proposed by them, a declaration of rights, in which are two articles providing, the one for the liberty of conscience, the other for the freedom of speech and of the press.

Similar recommendations having proceeded from a number of other States; and Congress, as has been seen, having in consequence thereof, and with a view to extend the ground of public confidence, proposed among other declaratory and restrictive clauses, a clause expressly securing the liberty of conscience and of the press; and Virginia having concurred in the ratifications which made them a part of the Constitution; it will remain with a candid public to decide, whether it would not mark an inconsistency and degeneracy, if an indifference were now shewn to a palpable violation of one of those rights, the freedom of the press; and to a precedent therein, which may be fatal to the other, the free exercise of religion.

That the precedent established by the violation of the former of these rights, may, as is affirmed by the resolution, be fatal to the latter, appears to be demonstrable, by a comparison of the grounds on which they respectively rest; and from the scope of reasoning, by which the power over the former has been vindicated.

First. Both of these rights, the liberty of conscience and of the press, rest equally on the original ground of not being delegated by the Constitution, and consequently withheld from the government. Any construction therefore, that would attack this original security for the one must have the like effect on the other.

Secondly. They are both equally secured by the supplement to the Constitution; being both included in the same amendment, made at the same time, and by the same authority. Any construction or argument then which would turn the amendment into a grant or acknowledgment of power with respect to the press, might be equally applied to the freedom of religion.

Thirdly. If it be admitted that the extent of the freedom of the press secured by the amendment, is to be measured by the common law on this subject; the same authority may be resorted to, for the standard which is to fix the extent of the "free exercise of religion." It cannot be necessary to say what this standard would be; whether the common law be taken solely as the unwritten, or as varied by the written, law of England.

Fourthly. If the words and phrases in the amendment, are to be considered as chosen with a studied discrimination, which yields an argument for a power over the press, under the limitation that its freedom be not abridged; the same argument results from the same consideration, for a power over the exercise of religion, under the limitation that its freedom be not prohibited.

For if Congress may regulate the freedom of the press, provided they do not abridge it: because it is said only, "they shall not abridge it;" and is not said, "they shall make no law respecting it:" the analogy of reasoning is conclusive, that Congress may *regulate* and even *abridge* the free exercise of religion; provided they do not *prohibit* it; because it is said only "they shall not prohibit it;" and is *not* said "they shall make no law *respecting* or no law *abridging* it."

The General Assembly were governed by the clearest reason, then, in considering the "Sedition Act," which legislates on the freedom of the press, as establishing a precedent that may be fatal to the liberty of conscience and it will be the duty of all, in proportion as they value the security of the latter, to take the alarm at every encroachment on the former.

The two concluding resolutions only remain to be examined. They are in the words following.

"That the good people of this commonwealth, having ever "felt, and continuing to feel the most sincere affection for "their brethren of the other States; the truest anxiety for estab- "lishing and perpetuating the union of all; and the most "scrupulous fidelity to that Constitution, which is the pledge "of mutual friendship, and the instrument of mutual happi- "ness; the General Assembly doth solemnly appeal to the like "dispositions in the other States, in confidence that they will "concur with this commonwealth in declaring, as it does "hereby declare, that the acts aforesaid, are unconstitutional; "and, that the necessary and proper measures will be taken "by each, for co-operating with this State, in maintaining un- "impaired, the authorities, rights, and liberties, reserved to the "States respectively, or to the People."

"That the Governor be desired, to transmit a copy of the "foregoing resolutions to the executive authority of each of "the other States, with a request that the same may be com- "municated to the Legislature thereof; and that a copy be fur- "nished to each of the Senators and Representatives represent- "ing this State in the Congress of the United States."

The fairness and regularity of the course of proceeding,

here pursued, have not protected it, against objections even from sources too respectable to be disregarded.

It has been said that it belongs to the judiciary of the United States, and not to the State legislatures, to declare the meaning of the Federal Constitution.

But a declaration that proceedings of the Federal government are not warranted by the Constitution, is a novelty neither among the citizens, nor among the legislatures of the States; nor are the citizens or the legislature of Virginia, singular in the example of it.

Nor can the declarations of either, whether affirming or denying the constitutionality of measures of the Federal government; or whether made before or after judicial decisions thereon, be deemed, in any point of view, an assumption of the office of the judge. The declarations in such cases, are expressions of opinion, unaccompanied with any other effect, than what they may produce on opinion, by exciting reflection. The expositions of the judiciary, on the other hand, are carried into immediate effect by force. The former may lead to a change in the legislative expression of the general will; possibly to a change in the opinion of the judiciary: the latter enforces the general will, whilst that will and that opinion continue unchanged.

And if there be no impropriety in declaring the unconstitutionality of proceedings in the Federal government; where can be the impropriety of communicating the declaration to other States, and inviting their concurrence in a like declaration? What is allowable for one, must be allowable for all; and a free communication among the States, where the Constitution imposes no restraint, is as allowable among the State governments, as among other public bodies, or private citizens. This consideration derives a weight, that cannot be denied to it, from the relation of the state legislatures, to the federal legislature, as the immediate constituents of one of its branches.

The legislatures of the States have a right also, to originate amendments to the Constitution, by a concurrence of two thirds of the whole number, in applications to Congress for the purpose. When new States are to be formed by a junction of two or more States, or parts of States, the legislatures of the States concerned, are, as well as Congress, to concur in the measure. The States have a right also, to enter into agreements, or compacts, with the consent of Congress. On all such cases, a communication among them, results from the object which is common to them.

It is lastly to be seen, whether the confidence expressed by the resolution, that the *necessary and proper measures*, would be taken by the other States, for co-operating with Virginia, in maintaining the rights reserved to the States, or to the people, be in any degree liable to the objections which have been raised against it.

If it be liable to objection, it must be, because either the object, or the means, are objectionable.

The object being to maintain what the Constitution has ordained, is in itself a laudable object.

The means are expressed in the terms "the necessary and proper measures." A proper object was to be pursued, by means both necessary and proper.

To find an objection then, it must be shewn, that some meaning was annexed to these general terms, which was not proper; and for this purpose, either that the means used by the General Assembly, were an example of improper means, or that there were no proper means to which the terms could refer.

In the example given by the State, of declaring the Alien and Sedition Acts to be unconstitutional, and of communicating the declaration to the other States, no trace of improper means has appeared. And if the other States had concurred in making a like declaration, supported too by the numerous applications flowing immediately from the people, it can scarcely be doubted, that these simple means would have been as sufficient, as they are unexceptionable.

It is no less certain, that other means might have been employed, which are strictly within the limits of the Constitution. The legislatures of the States might have made a direct representation to Congress, with a view to obtain a rescinding of the two offensive acts; or they might have represented to their respective senators in Congress, their wish, that two thirds thereof would propose an explanatory amendment to the Constitution; or two thirds of themselves, if such had been their option, might, by an application to Congress, have obtained a convention for the same object.

These several means, though not equally eligible in themselves, nor probably, to the States, were all constitutionally open for consideration. And if the General Assembly, after declaring the two acts to be unconstitutional, the first and most obvious proceeding on the subject, did not undertake to point out to the other States, a choice among the farther measures that might become necessary and proper, the reserve will not be misconstrued by liberal minds, into any culpable imputation.

These observations appear to form a satisfactory reply, to every objection which is not founded on a misconception of the terms, employed in the resolutions. There is one other however, which may be of too much importance not to be added. It cannot be forgotten, that among the arguments addressed to those, who apprehended danger to liberty, from the establishment of the general government over so great a country; the appeal was emphatically made to the intermediate existence of the State governments, between the people and that government, to the vigilance with which they would descry the first symptoms of usurpation, and to the promptitude with which they would sound the alarm to the public. This argument was probably not without its effect; and if it was a proper one, then, to recommend the establishment of the Constitution; it must be a proper one now, to assist in its interpretation.

The only part of the two concluding resolutions, that remain to be noticed, is the repetition in the first, of that warm affection to the union and its members, and of that scrupulous fidelity to the Constitution which have been invaribly felt by the people of this State. As the proceedings were introduced with these sentiments, they could not be more properly closed, than in the same manner. Should there be any so far misled, as to call in question the sincerity of these professions, whatever regret may be excited by the error, the General Assembly cannot descend into a discussion of it. Those who have listened to the suggestion, can only be left to their own recollection, of the part which this State has borne in the establishment of our national independence; in the establishment of our national Constitution; and in maintaining under it, the authority and laws of the union, without a single exception of internal resistance or commotion. By recurring to these facts, they will be able to convince themselves, that the representatives of the people of Virginia must be above the necessity of opposing any other shield to attacks on their national patriotism, than their own consciousness and the justice of an enlightened public; who will perceive in the resolutions themselves, the strongest evidence of attachment both to the Constitution and to the union, since it is only by maintaining the different governments and departments within their respective limits, that the blessings of either can be perpetuated.

The extensive view of the subject thus taken by the committee, has led them to report to the house, as the result of the whole, the following resolution.

Resolved, That the General Assembly, having carefully and respectfully attended to the proceedings of a number of the States, in answer to their resolutions of December 21, 1798, and having accurately and fully re-examined and re-considered the latter, find it to be their indispensable duty to adhere to the same, as founded in truth, as consonant with the Constitution, and as conducive to its preservation; and more especially to be their duty, to renew, as they do hereby renew, their protest against "the Alien and Sedition Acts," as palpable and alarming infractions of the Constitution.

☆   ☆   ☆

A motion was then made, and the question being put, that the House do agree to the report of the committee?

It passed in the affirmative.

"On the state of the commonwealth;" being read,

Ordered, that the same be put off until to-morrow.

And then the House adjourned 'till to-morrow morning ten o'clock.